VERONA
INTERNATIONAL

11
12
13

OCTOBER

TATTOO
EXPO 2024

THE ALLSTARS
TATTOO By Emilio
CONVENTION Gonzalez

15 USA
16 MIAMI
17 NOVEMBER

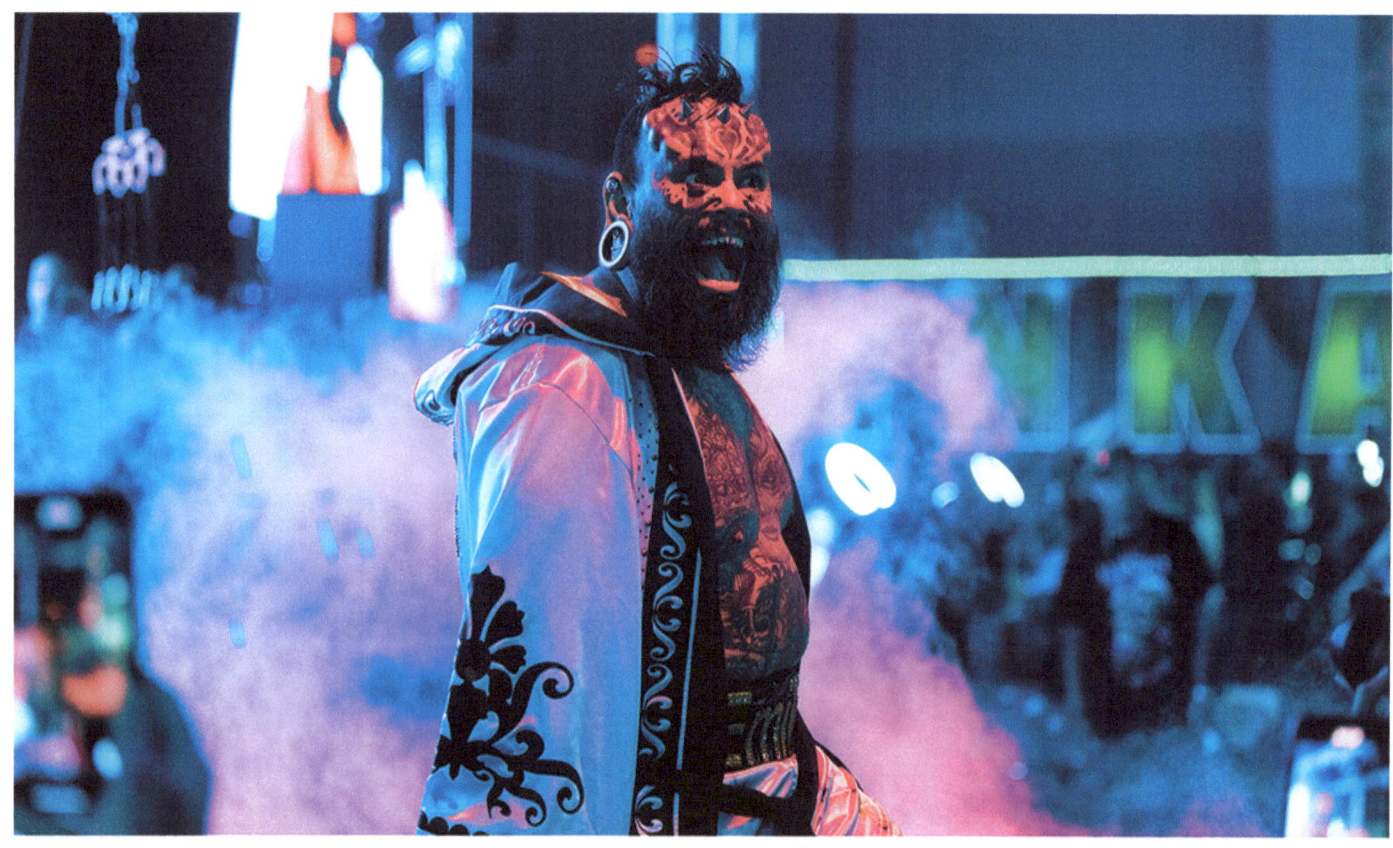

By now, you have probably heard all about the event that changed the game for tattoo conventions in the United States. Just in case you are one of the few that been living under a rock, we have the full recap for you.

The All Stars Tattoo Convention in Miami, held from September 29 to October 1, was a vibrant celebration of ink, creativity, and the global tattoo community. Gathering the most exceptional tattoo artists from around the world, the convention showcased the incredible talent and diverse styles that make the world of body art so fascinating. From traditional designs to cutting-edge innovations, attendees were treated to a visual feast that highlighted the evolving nature of tattoo artistry.

One of the standout performances at the convention was the show producer himself, El Monstro, Emilio Gonzalez, and his insane suspension act. Gonzalez, known for pushing the boundaries of body suspension, left audiences awe-struck with his daring performance. His suspension act not only demonstrated the physical and mental strength required for such a feat but also showcased the artistry involved in turning the human body into a canvas for unconventional

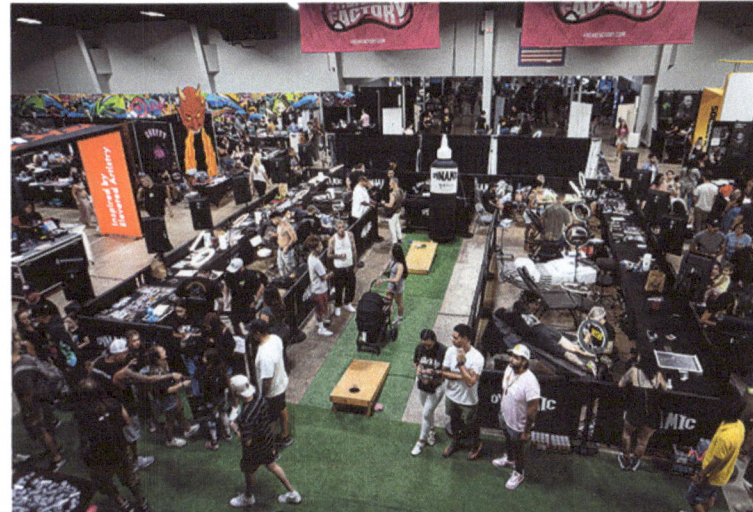

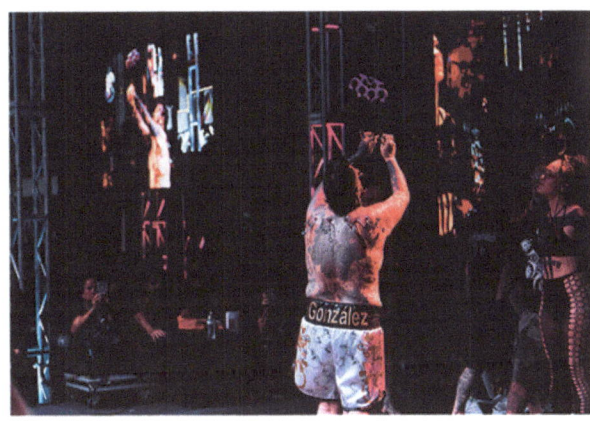

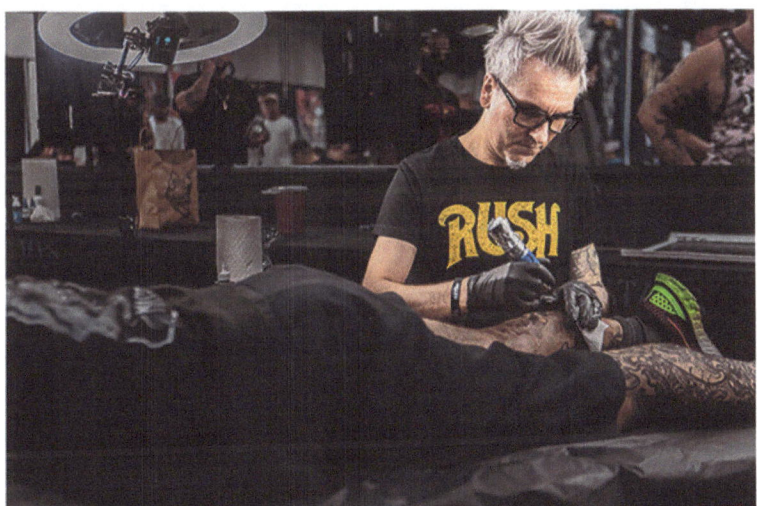

expression. The gasps and applause from the crowd were a testament to the convention's commitment to pushing the envelope and embracing the avant-garde aspects of tattoo culture.

Beyond the inked masterpieces and gravity-defying acts, the All Stars Tattoo Convention provided a platform for artists and enthusiasts to connect, share ideas, and appreciate the rich tapestry of tattooing traditions worldwide. It served as a melting pot of cultures, where artists exchanged techniques, stories, and inspirations, fostering a sense of community within the global tattoo scene. As the convention came to a close, it left an indelible mark on Miami, proving that tattoo artistry is not just skin deep; it is a dynamic and evolving form of self-expression that continues to captivate and unite people from all walks of life.

Heavy hitters were everywhere at the event. The All Stars Tattoo Convention in Miami welcomed a constellation of legendary tattoo artists, each contributing to the event's status as a pinnacle of inked artistry. The presence of luminaries like Robert Hernandez, whose dark and intricate designs have garnered international acclaim, added an extra layer of prestige to the convention. Accompanying him were renowned artists such as Robert Pho, Yomico Moreno, Darwin Enriquez, Stefano Alacantra, Big Meas, Yeyo, Flaks, Fred, Sergey Shenko, Steve Butcher, Horihui, Bong Tatau, Dave Paulo, Arlo DiSilva, Bolo, Victor Portugal, Victor Chil, Rember and countless other giant names of the industry-

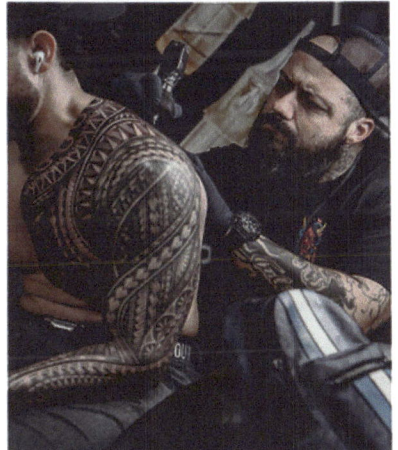

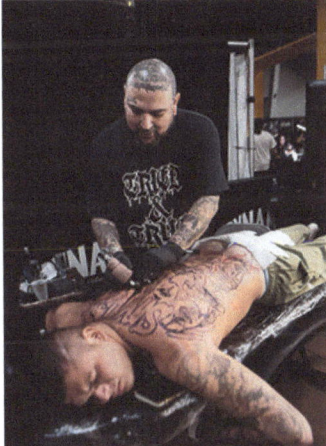

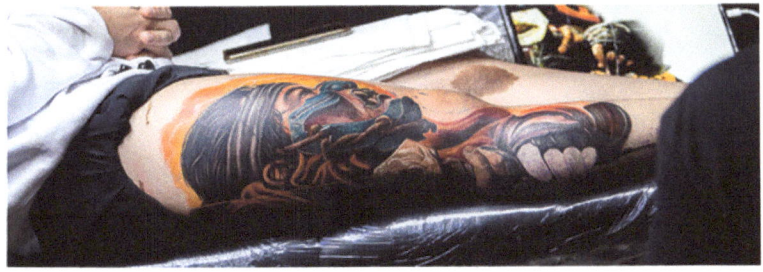

The convention served as a unique opportunity for attendees to witness live demonstrations, engage in discussions, and even get inked by these titans of the tattoo world. From Hernandez's ethereal realism to Moreno's masterful portraits and Alacantra's fusion of geometric precision and cultural motifs, the diverse styles represented highlighted the kaleidoscopic nature of contemporary tattoo art. The convergence of such iconic figures under one roof at the All Stars Tattoo Convention underscored its significance as a global epicenter for the convergence of talent, innovation, and passion within the vibrant world of body art.

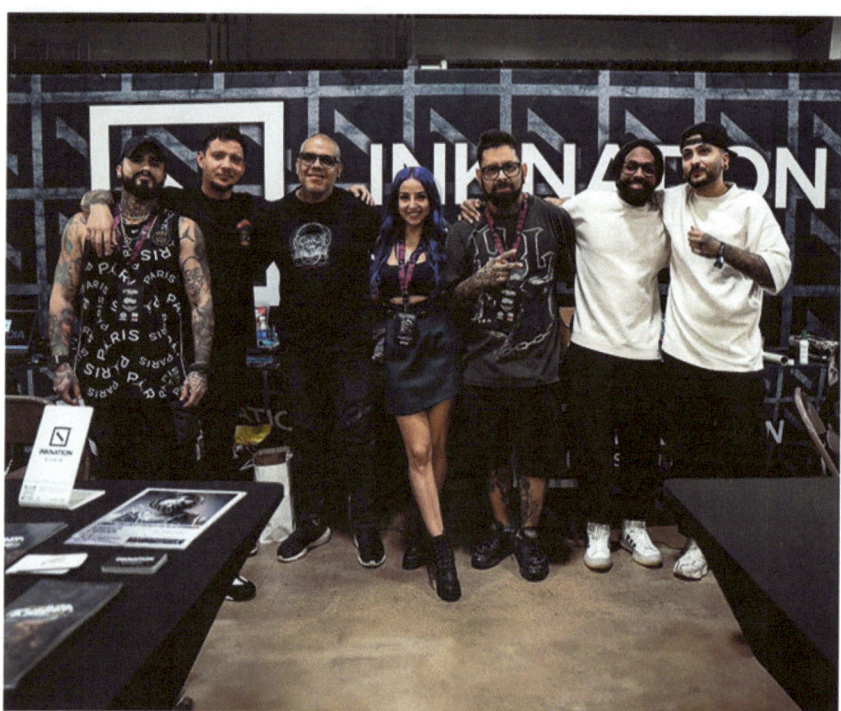

Another game changer was the inclusion and huge presence from the body modification world, which comes as no surprise being that the events host and owner is arguably the biggest name in body modification globally. The All Stars Tattoo Convention in Miami transcended the boundaries of conventional body art by attracting a gathering of influential body modification enthusiasts. Among the notable attendees were luminaries like The Black Alien, whose avant-garde approach to body modification challenges traditional norms and inspires a new wave of self-expression. Rob Bucholtz, celebrated for his world

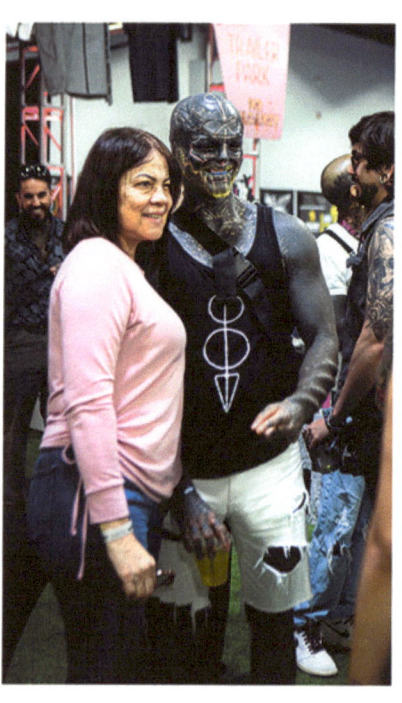
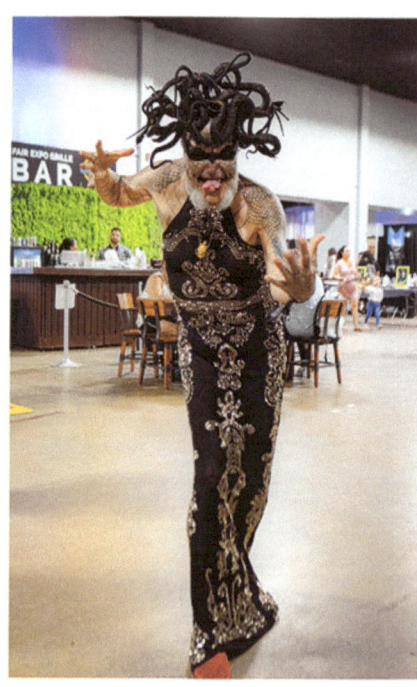

record amount of piercings, tattoo coverage and intricate body modifications, added a unique flair to the event. Matt Gone, known for his striking checkerboard body pattern, and Lady Medusa, an icon in the body modification community, were also present, captivating audiences with their bold and transformative choices.

The convention further embraced diversity with the attendance of names like Kala Kawai and Modified Apparition, recognized for pushing the boundaries of dermal implants and other cutting-edge modifications, and Gato Moreno, whose distinctive facial tattoos and body alterations make him a standout figure in the global body modification scene. Their presence not only celebrated individuality but also underscored the inclusive spirit of the All Stars Tattoo Convention, where enthusiasts from various corners of the body modification spectrum converged to share their stories, ideas, and passion for pushing the limits of physical self-expression. The event became a melting pot of creativity, fostering a sense of community that transcended the boundaries of traditional tattoo artistry.

THE CONTEST

The All Stars Tattoo Convention elevated the excitement by hosting extensive tattoo contests that set a new standard in the industry. Judged by the most respected artists in their respective fields, these contests showcased a dazzling array of talent across various categories. Emilio took on the role of the MC, infusing the contests with energy and charisma. Industry insiders are buzzing about the unmatched fairness and level of talent displayed throughout the competitions.

One innovative aspect that garnered widespread acclaim was the meticulous separation of categories into healed and fresh tattoos, ensuring a comprehensive evaluation of skill and artistry. The groundbreaking decision to restrict contest entries to artists with booths at the show added an extra layer of fairness and integrity. This unique approach not only ensured that every participant was actively involved in the convention but also leveled the playing field, eliminating any potential bias. The result was a showcase of unparalleled talent, a testament to the organizers' commitment to fostering an environment where excellence and innovation in tattoo artistry could be rightfully celebrated. The All Stars Tattoo Convention's approach to judging contests has set a new industry standard, sparking conversations about its fairness and paving the way for future conventions to follow suit.

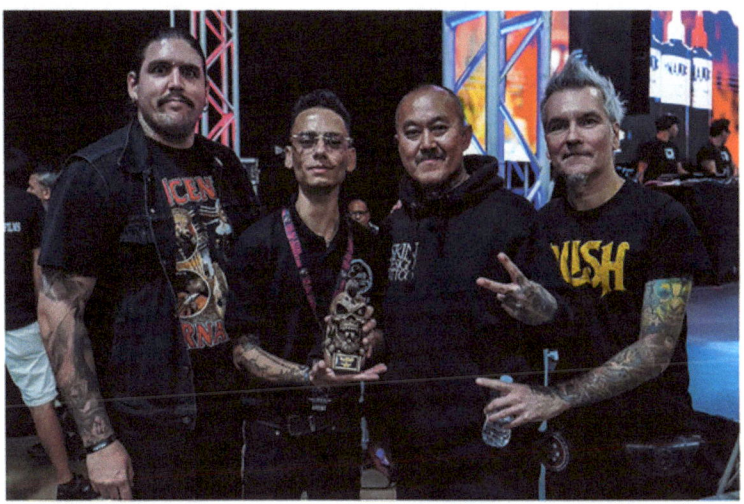

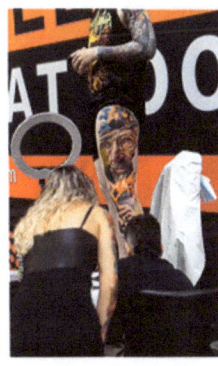

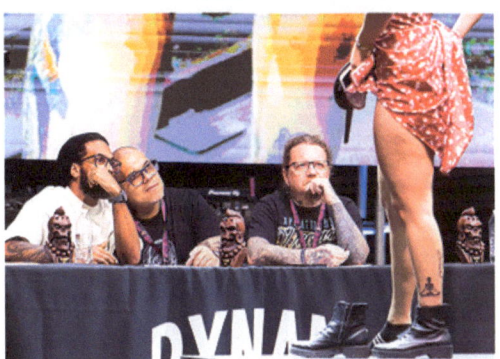

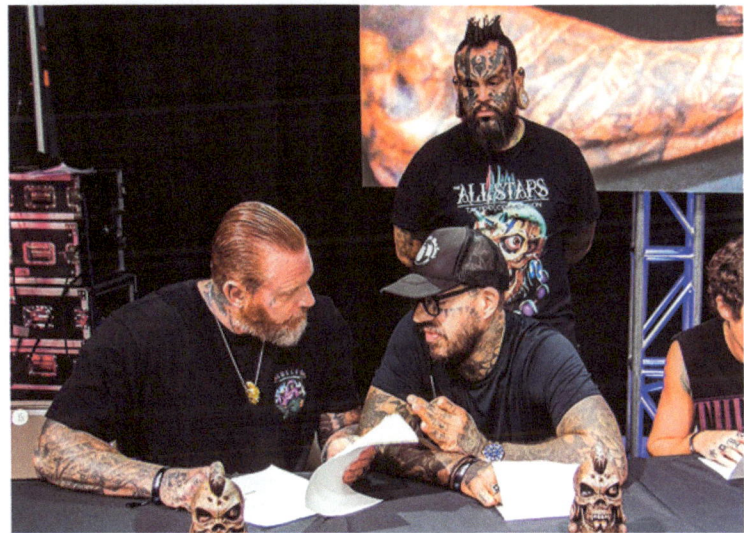

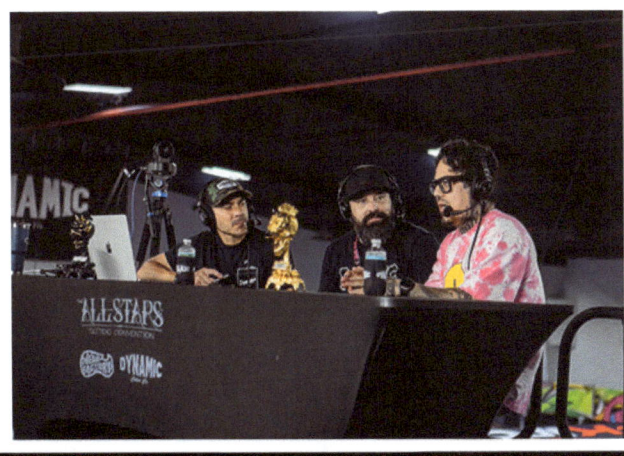

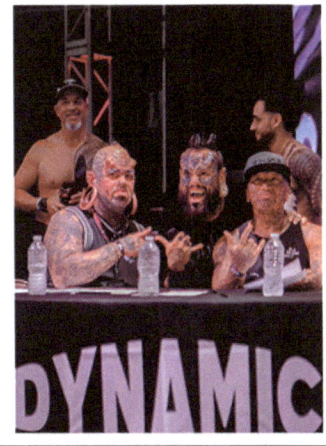

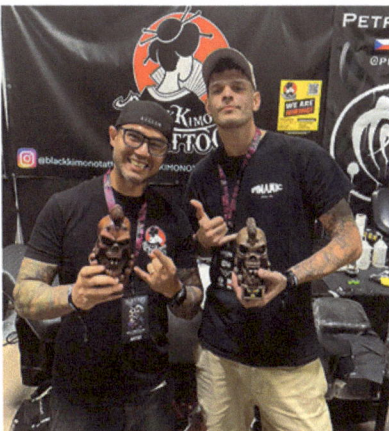

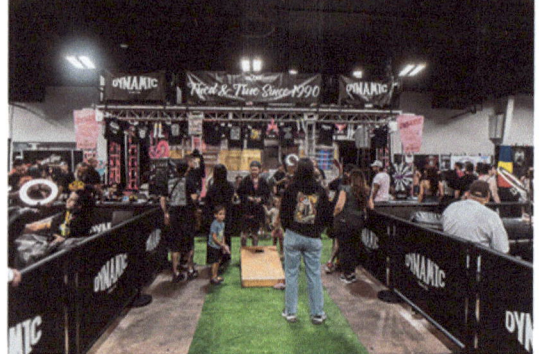
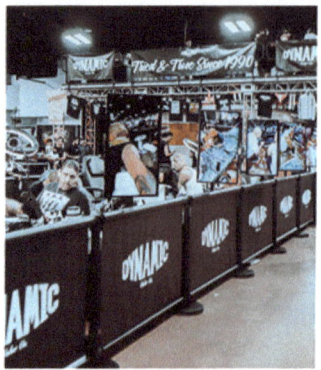

The success of the All Stars Tattoo Convention was undoubtedly bolstered by the invaluable support of its sponsors, who played a pivotal role in bringing the event to life. Dynamic Color, known for its high-quality and vibrant inks, provided artists with the essential pigments needed to create stunning and long-lasting designs. Freak Factory Tattoo Supply, another key sponsor, contributed to the convention's seamless operation by ensuring that artists had access to top-notch equipment and supplies. From needles to machines, their commitment to supplying only quality products underscored the convention's dedication to excellence in every aspect of the tattooing process. Additionally, FK Irons Tattoo Machines, a renowned name in the industry, showcased their cutting-edge technology, demonstrating the innovative strides being made in the world of tattoo machines. These sponsors not only demonstrated their commitment to the art of tattooing but also played an integral role in elevating the All Stars Tattoo Convention into a truly world-class event. Their support allowed the convention to provide an enriching experience for both artists and attendees, further solidifying their place as champions of the global tattoo community.

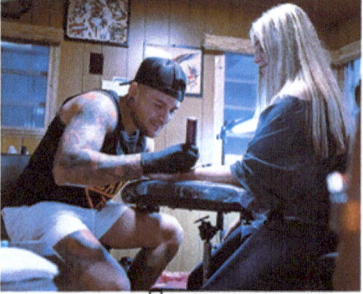
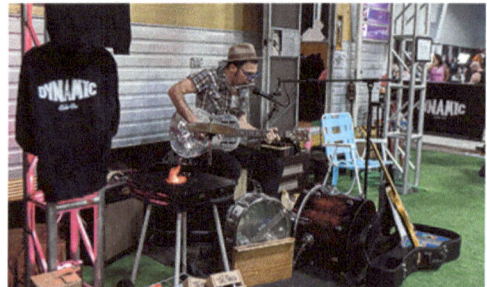

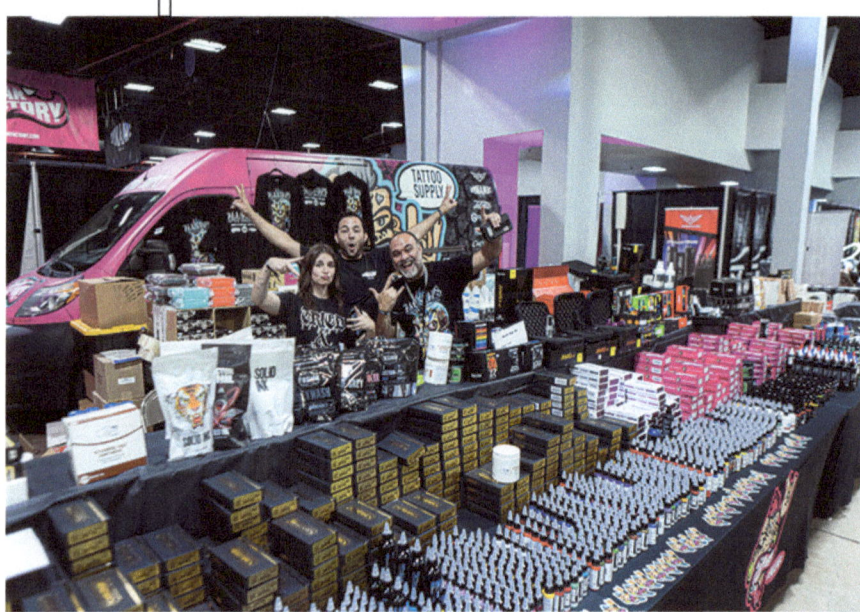

The Dynamic Color booth stood out as a hub of innovation and entertainment, offering patrons a truly immersive experience. The booth featured a dazzling display of creativity with 12 skilled artists, each equipped with mounted TVs showcasing mesmerizing close-up GoPro footage of their intricate tattooing processes. This unique setup allowed attendees to witness the meticulous details and techniques employed by these artists, providing an up-close and personal view that added a new dimension to the appreciation of tattoo artistry.

Adding to the booth's allure was its unconventional setting as a vintage trailer park-a nod to old Florida charm. This inventive layout not only provided a nostalgic atmosphere but also created an intimate and welcoming space for visitors to engage with the artists and their craft. The second story of the trailer park doubled as a live-stream booth, hosting interviews with renowned artists and providing lively commentary on the weekend's activities. This dynamic setup transformed the Dynamic Color booth into a captivating hub of activity, blending the traditions of tattoo artistry with modern technology and a touch of retro flair. It became a central focal point for attendees seeking both inspiration and a deeper connection to the vibrant world of tattoo culture.

The All Stars Tattoo Convention in Miami wasn't just a visual feast for tattoo enthusiasts; it was a sensory carnival that included non-stop entertainment throughout the weekend. Attendees were treated to an eclectic mix of musical performances, with live bands and DJs, thrilling stunt shows by Auzzy Blood and Indigo Fox setting the stage on fire with their energetic daredevil performances. The convention took the experience to the next level with the inclusion of a Polynesian fire dancing troupe, who traveled all the way from Tahiti, adding a touch of exotic flair to the festivities. Their mesmerizing fire dance performances illuminated the night, creating an enchanting ambiance that transported attendees to far-off, tropical realms.

In addition to the rhythmic beats and fiery displays, multiple other dancers adorned the stage, showcasing their talents in various styles. The diverse array of performances, ranging from traditional to risqué dance forms, contributed to the dynamic and inclusive atmosphere of the event. Whether patrons were getting inked, exploring booths, or simply enjoying the vibrant ambiance, the non-stop entertainment served as a sensory backdrop that enhanced the overall experience of the All Stars Tattoo Convention. It wasn't just an event; it was a celebration of creativity, culture, and the shared passion for the art of expression in all its forms.

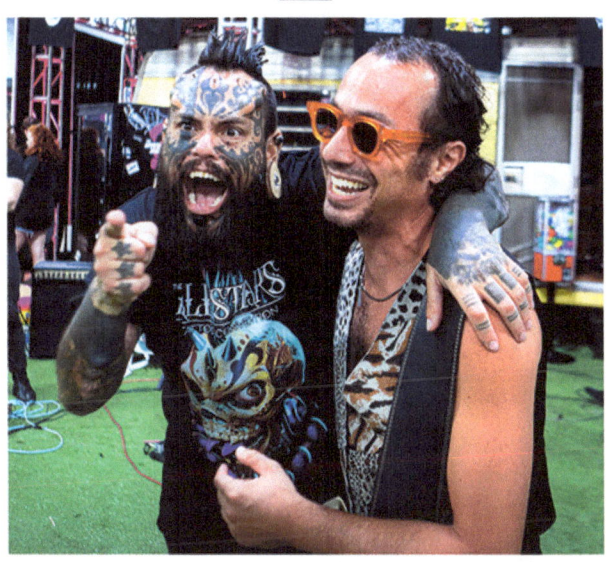

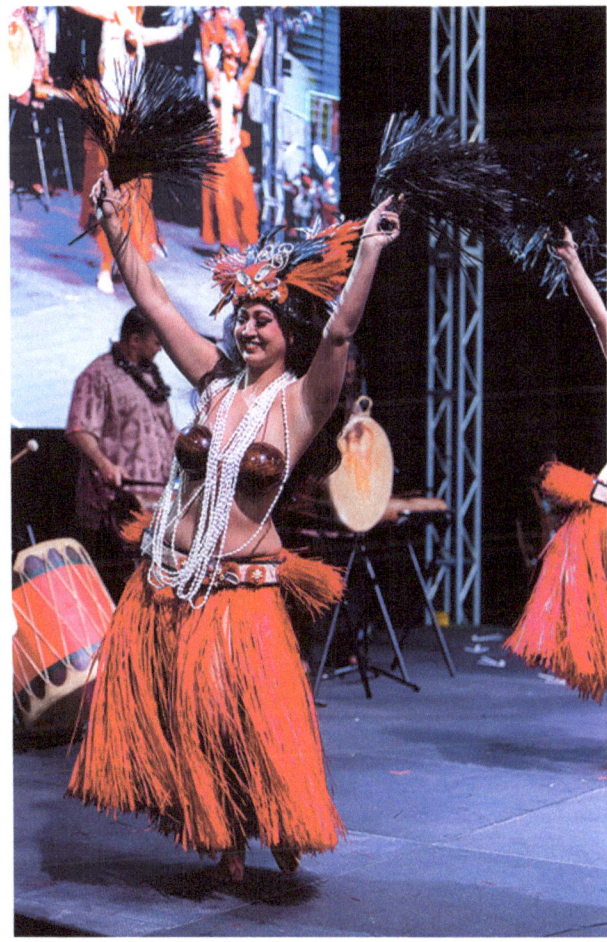

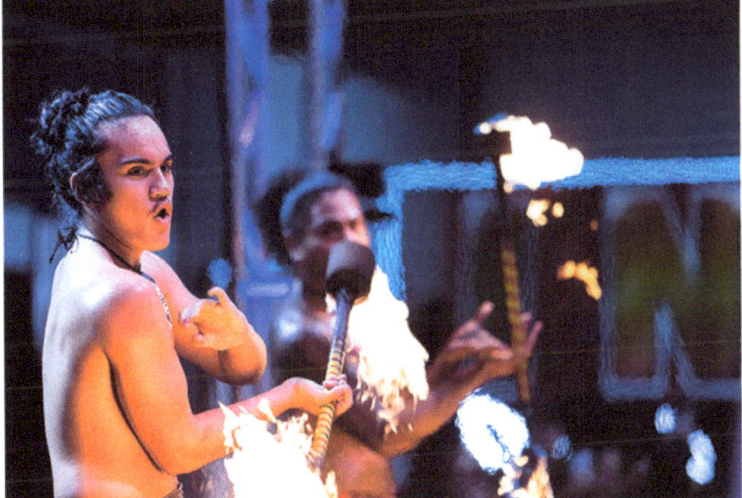

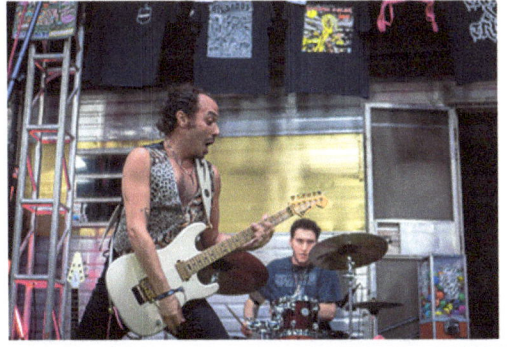

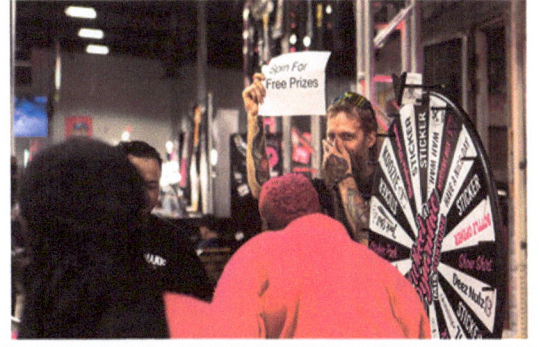

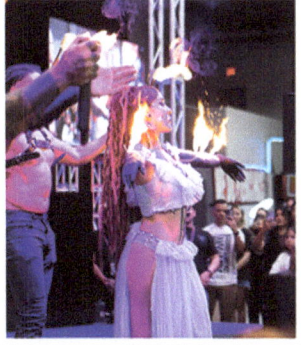

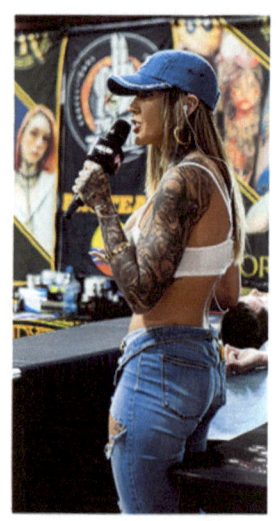

Positioned at the front entrance, Golden305 worked his artistic magic on a colossal graffiti piece that served as a dynamic and evolving focal point at the entrance to the event. The live painting session not only added a bold and visually striking element to the convention but also paid homage to the city's rich cultural tapestry. Golden305, known for his mastery in the world of street art, infused the entrance with his signature style, creating a piece that became a captivating conversation starter among attendees. As the vibrant hues and intricate details unfolded in real-time, it became a living testament to the fusion of various art forms, from tattoos to graffiti, all converging under the Miami sun. The live graffiti installation by Golden305 at the All Stars Tattoo Convention exemplified the event's commitment to showcasing diverse artistic expressions and creating an immersive experience that extended beyond the confines of traditional tattoo conventions. It not only welcomed attendees with a burst of color but also underscored the dynamic and ever-evolving nature of the creative community in Miami.

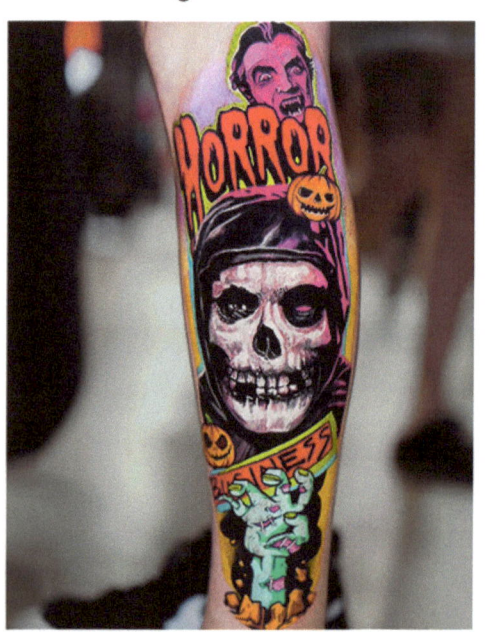
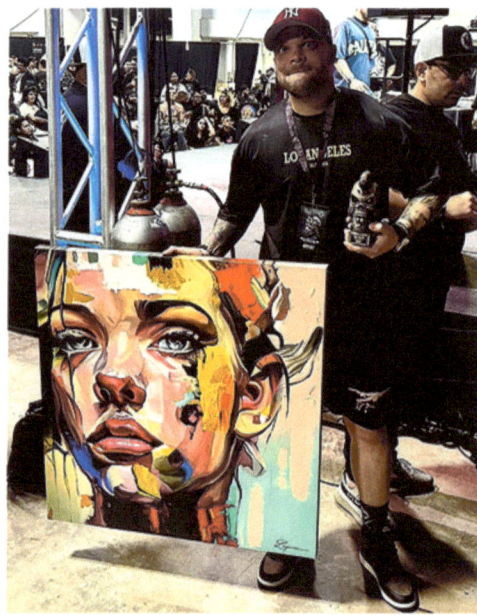
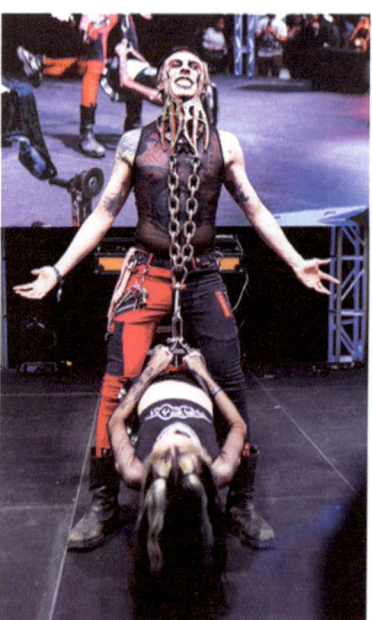

As the curtain falls on the spectacular All Stars Tattoo Convention in Miami, the echoes of creativity and camaraderie linger, leaving attendees with unforgettable memories. Looking ahead, the anticipation for next year's event in November 2024 is already building. Promising to be bigger, better, and brimming with even more layers of art and music entertainment, the organizers are committed to raising the bar once again. Envision a convergence of global tattoo luminaries, renowned artists, and innovative performers coming together to create an immersive experience that transcends the boundaries of conventional conventions.

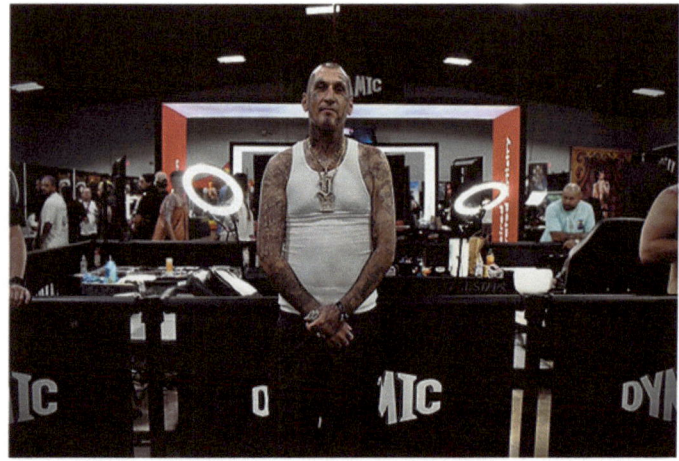
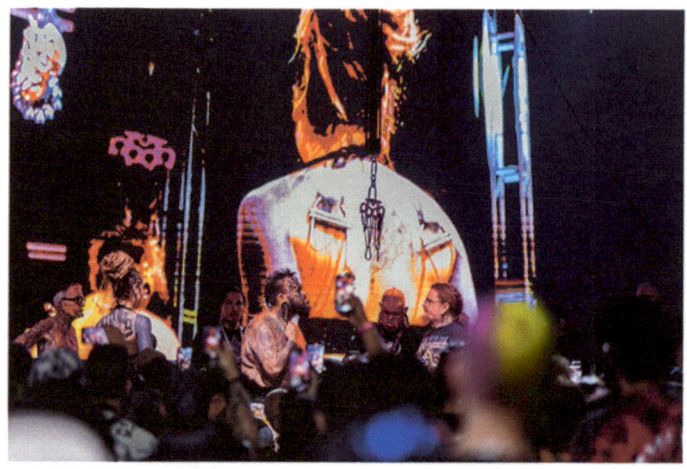

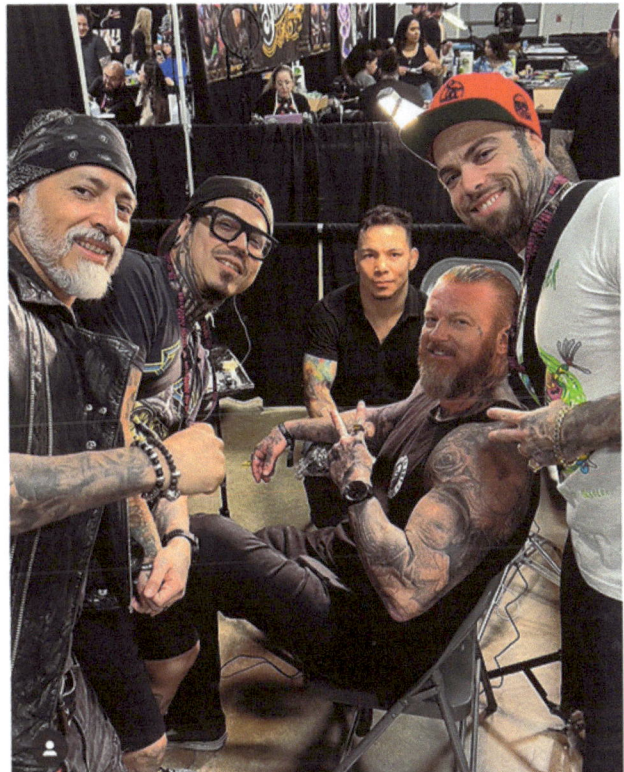

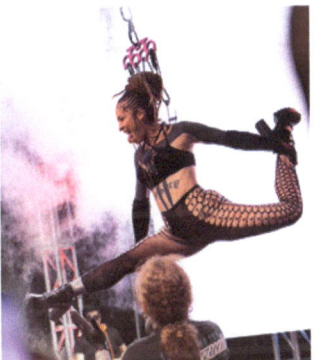

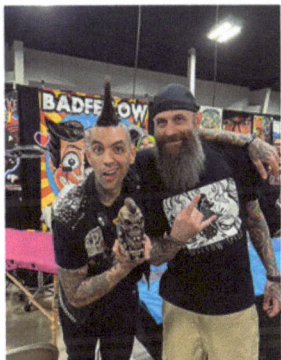

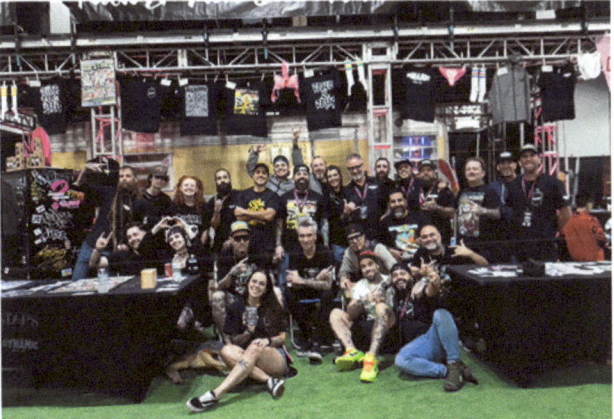

JURY AND WINNERS

Jurys:
Robert Hernandez
Robert Pho
Victor Chill
Freed
Yomico Moreno
Steve Butcher
Mr Reyes Ink
Horihui
Horiei
Century_tattoo
Myke Chambers

Big Meas:
Flaks32g
Shane O'Neil
Darwin Enriquez
Roberto Carlos
Richard Arthur
Isnar Bravo
Russel
Crush Capitan
Sergey Shanko
Daria Pirojenko
Bolo
Bong Tatau
Noho Tatau
Among others...

Best Of Show :
Yaniel mieres

Best Artwork:
Bolo

Color Infused:
Michele Serrano

Best Anime Color:
Peter hilgers

Collaboration:
Dany luz y
Naboka anastasiia

Water Color:
Chris swenski

Craziest Tattoo:
Yunior Luna

Neotraditional:
Coes ink

Best Color Realism:
Yeyo

Color Tattoo:
Bobby Bedfellow

Free Hand Polynesian:
Juliano Torres

Free Hand Geometric:
Juliano Torres

Large Black and Grey:
Obuzzz

Best Saturday:
Victor art Garcia

Lettering:
Petr Matej

Oriental Cured:
Gregos

Oriental Fresh:
Marco artt

Among others...

With the success of this year's groundbreaking features and the pulse of creativity still resonating, the All Stars Tattoo Convention is poised to become an annual rendezvous that not only celebrates the art of ink but continues to push the boundaries of what a tattoo convention can be. Mark your calendars for a November spectacle that promises to redefine the standards of the tattoo industry and captivate enthusiasts from around the world. The journey continues, and the stage is set for a celebration that will leave an indelible mark on the tapestry of global tattoo culture.

MANHATTAN - NY - EEUU - @jac_alonso

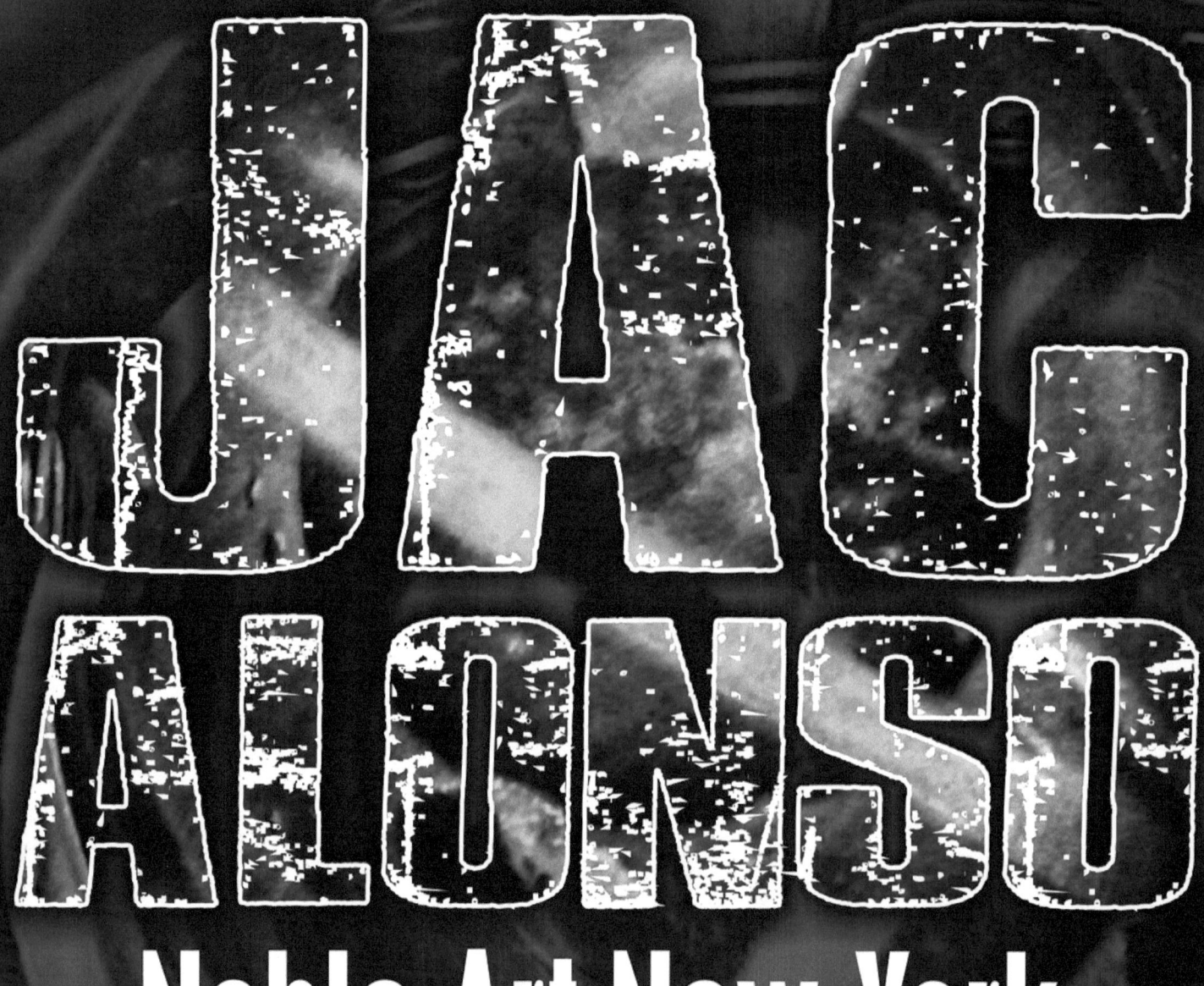

JAC ALONSO

Noble Art New York

Jac Alonso is a distinguished tattoo artist based in Manhattan, New York. Coming from Sevilla, Spain, Transitioning from a career in commerce in 2010, he pursued his passion for art through tattooing. Specializing in black and grey realism, Alonso's work captivates with its depth and emotion. His journey in New York has been marked by continuous growth and recognition, including to prestigious tattoo conventions like the Empire State Tattoo Convention. Focused on exceeding client expectations and pushing artistic boundaries, Jac Alonso is dedicated to furthering his impact within the vibrant tattoo community of Manhattan.

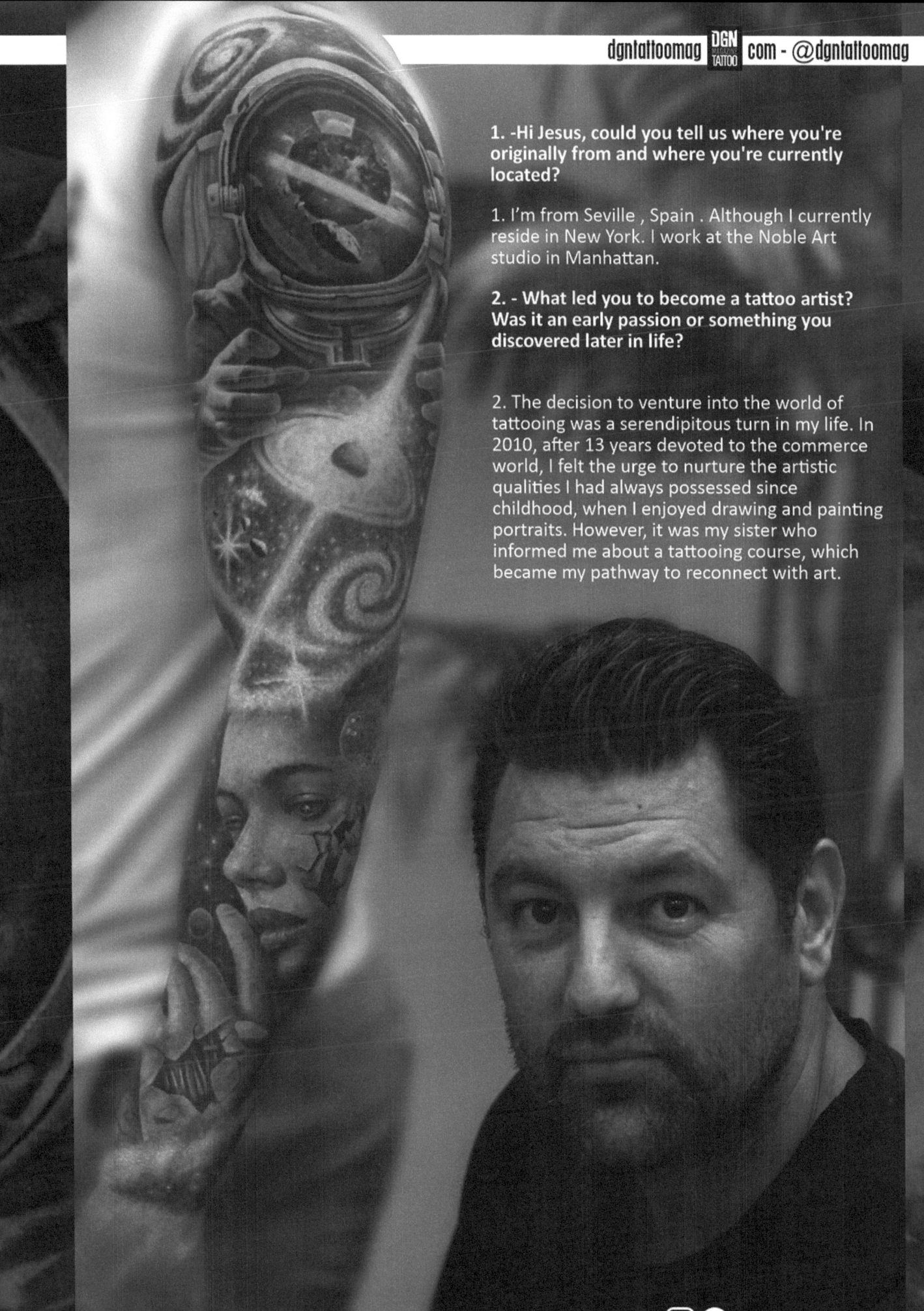

1. -Hi Jesus, could you tell us where you're originally from and where you're currently located?

1. I'm from Seville , Spain . Although I currently reside in New York. I work at the Noble Art studio in Manhattan.

2. - What led you to become a tattoo artist? Was it an early passion or something you discovered later in life?

2. The decision to venture into the world of tattooing was a serendipitous turn in my life. In 2010, after 13 years devoted to the commerce world, I felt the urge to nurture the artistic qualities I had always possessed since childhood, when I enjoyed drawing and painting portraits. However, it was my sister who informed me about a tattooing course, which became my pathway to reconnect with art.

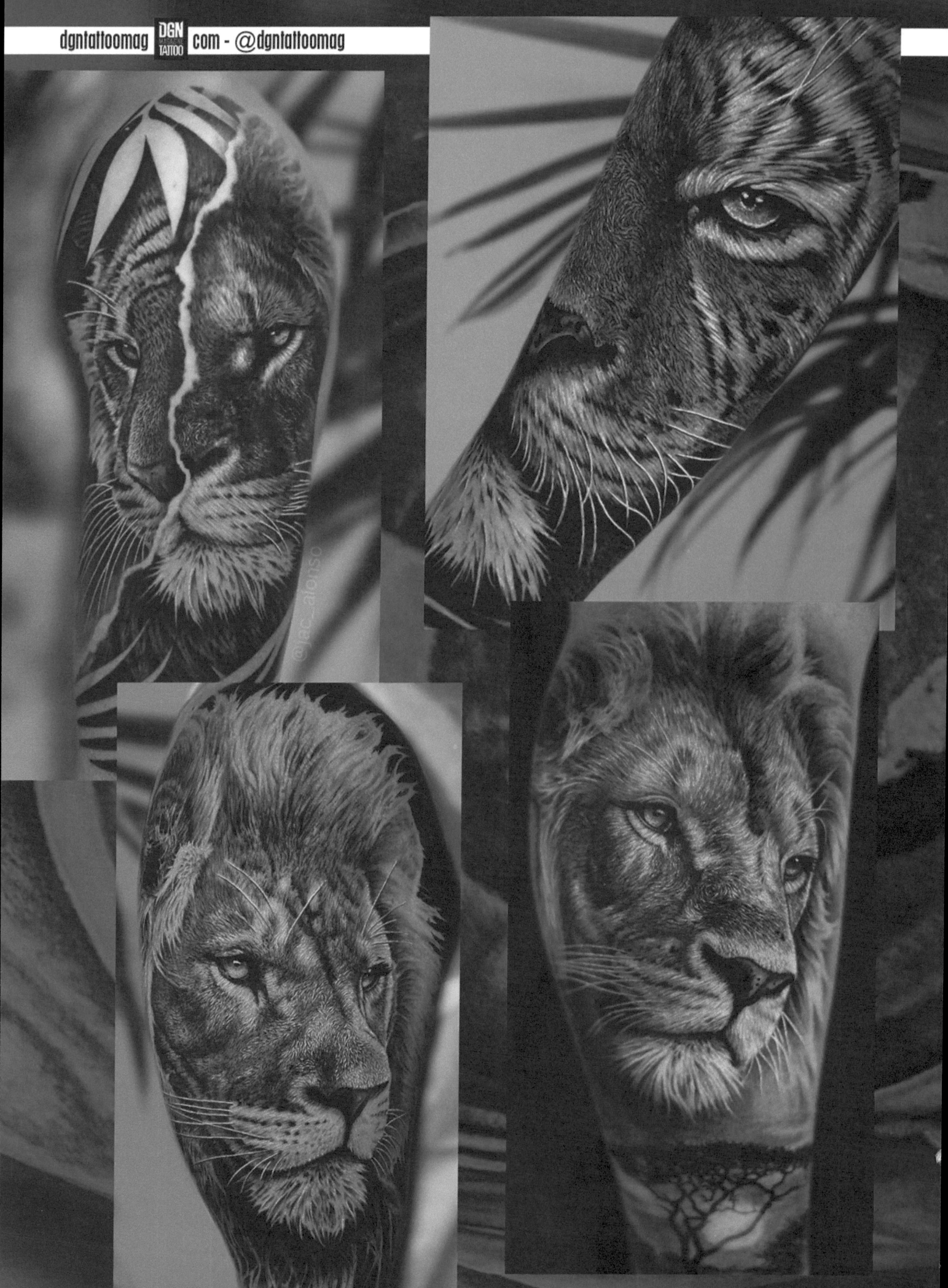

3. - How were your first steps in the tattoo industry? Do you remember your first professional tattoo?

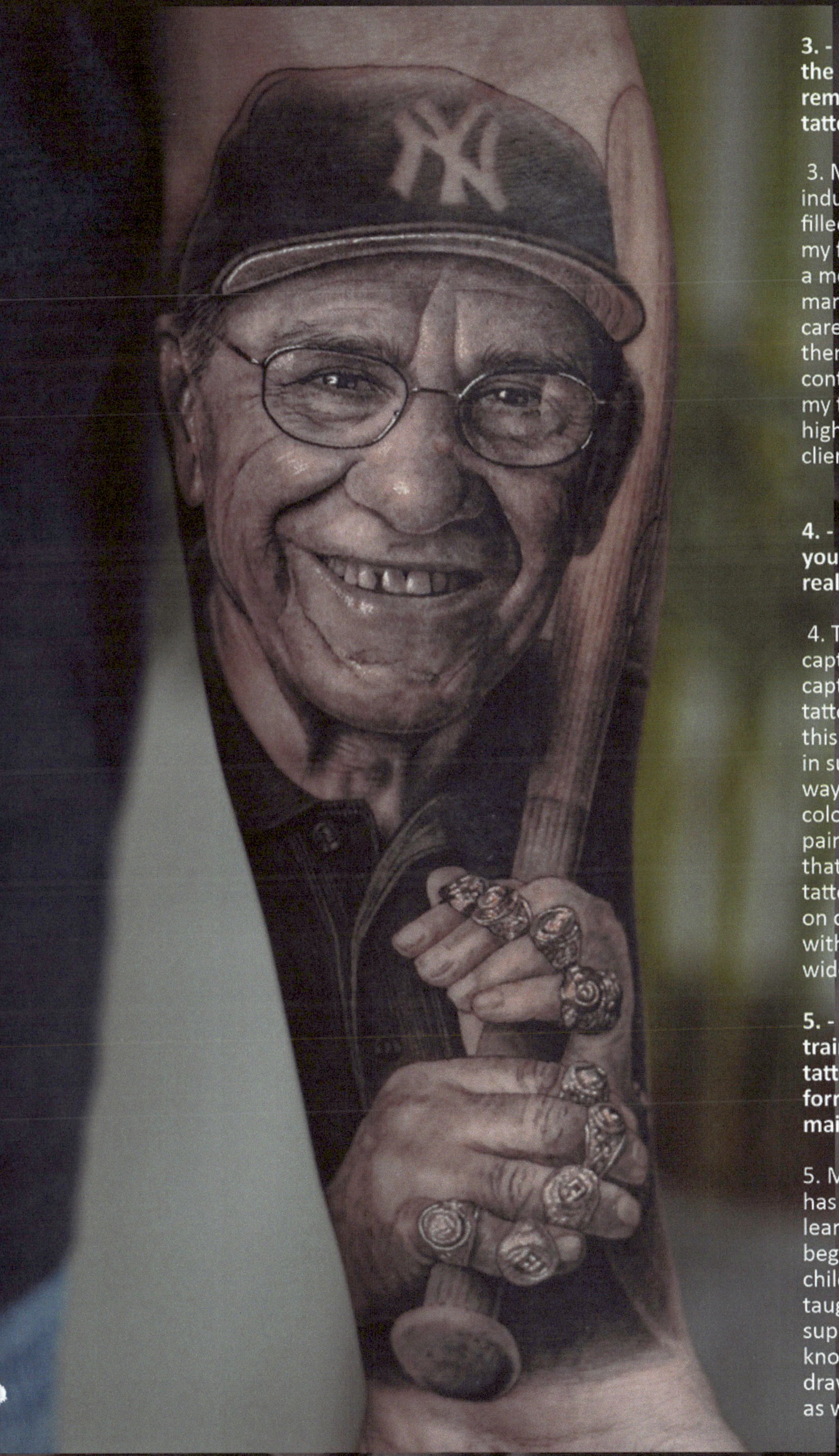

3. My initial steps into the tattoo industry were exhilarating and filled with learning. I vividly recall my first professional tattoo; it was a memorable moment that marked the beginning of my career as a tattoo artist. Since then, I have been and will continue to work on perfecting my technique to deliver the highest quality possible to my clients.

4. - What specifically attracted you to the style of black and grey realism in your tattoos?

4. The black and grey realism captivated me with its ability to capture depth and emotion in tattoos. I'm fascinated by how this style can bring images to life in such an intense and enduring way. Despite having worked with color in other techniques like oil painting or using pastels, I find that focusing on black and grey in tattoos allows me to concentrate on composition and details without being distracted by a wide color palette.

5. - Could you tell us about your training and education as a tattoo artist? Did you receive formal training or were you mainly self-taught?

5. My journey as a tattoo artist has been a blend of self-taught learning and formal education. I began my passion for art as a child, drawing portraits as a self-taught artist. Later on, my parents supported me in expanding my knowledge and skills through drawing and oil painting classes, as well as attending the School of

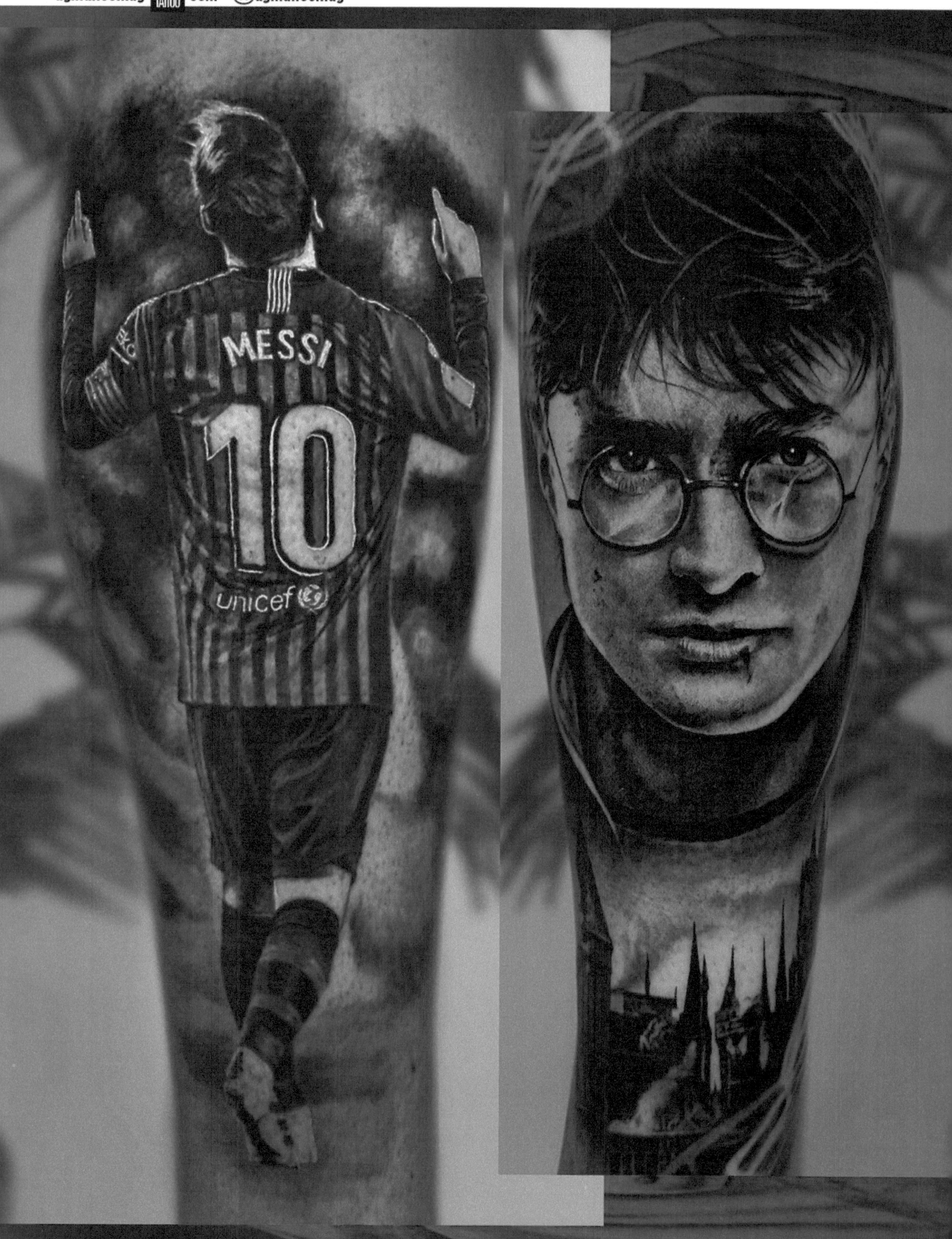

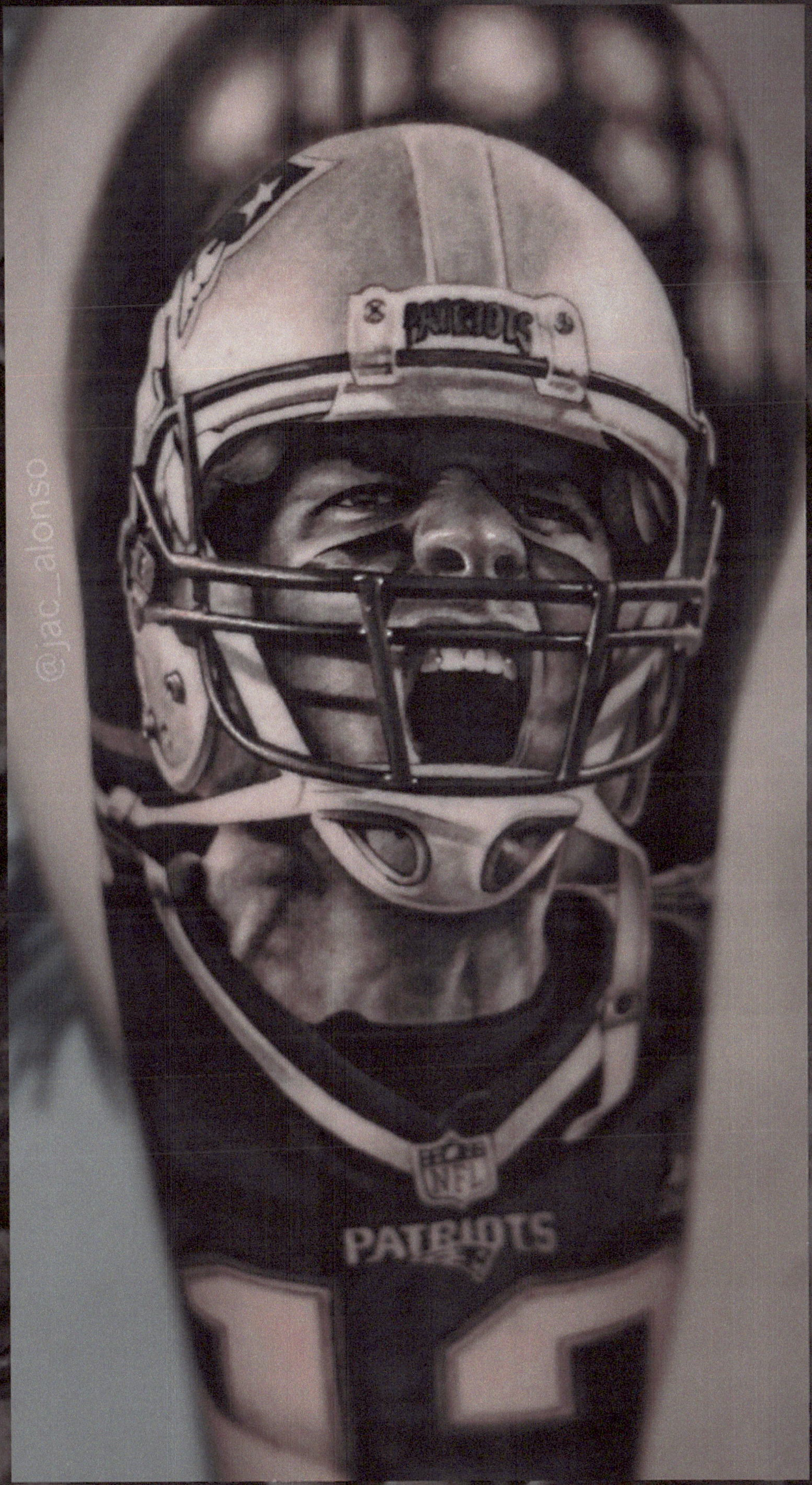

@jac_alonso

Arts and Crafts in Seville for several years. It was there where I developed a deeper understanding of fundamental artistic techniques. Subsequently, when I decided to delve into the world of tattooing, I supplemented my education with specific courses and practical learning from experienced tattoo artists. This combination of self-taught experiences and formal training has been crucial in shaping my development as a tattoo artist.

6. - Do you have any role models or artists who have inspired you in your career as a tattoo artist? What specific elements do you admire in their work?

6. Yes, throughout my career as a tattoo artist, I've had several role models and artists who have inspired me. I've had the opportunity to attend seminars and learn from leading artists in the tattoo industry. These artists have been a great source of inspiration for me and have influenced my own style and approach to tattooing.

7. - What has been the biggest challenge you've faced as a tattoo artist so far? And what has been your greatest achievement?

7. My greatest challenge lies in continually refining my technique and expanding my creativity to deliver tattoos to my clients that exceed their expectations. My greatest achievement has been to make a living from my passion. Since then, my focus has always been on artistic excellence, client satisfaction, and continuous growth as an artist.

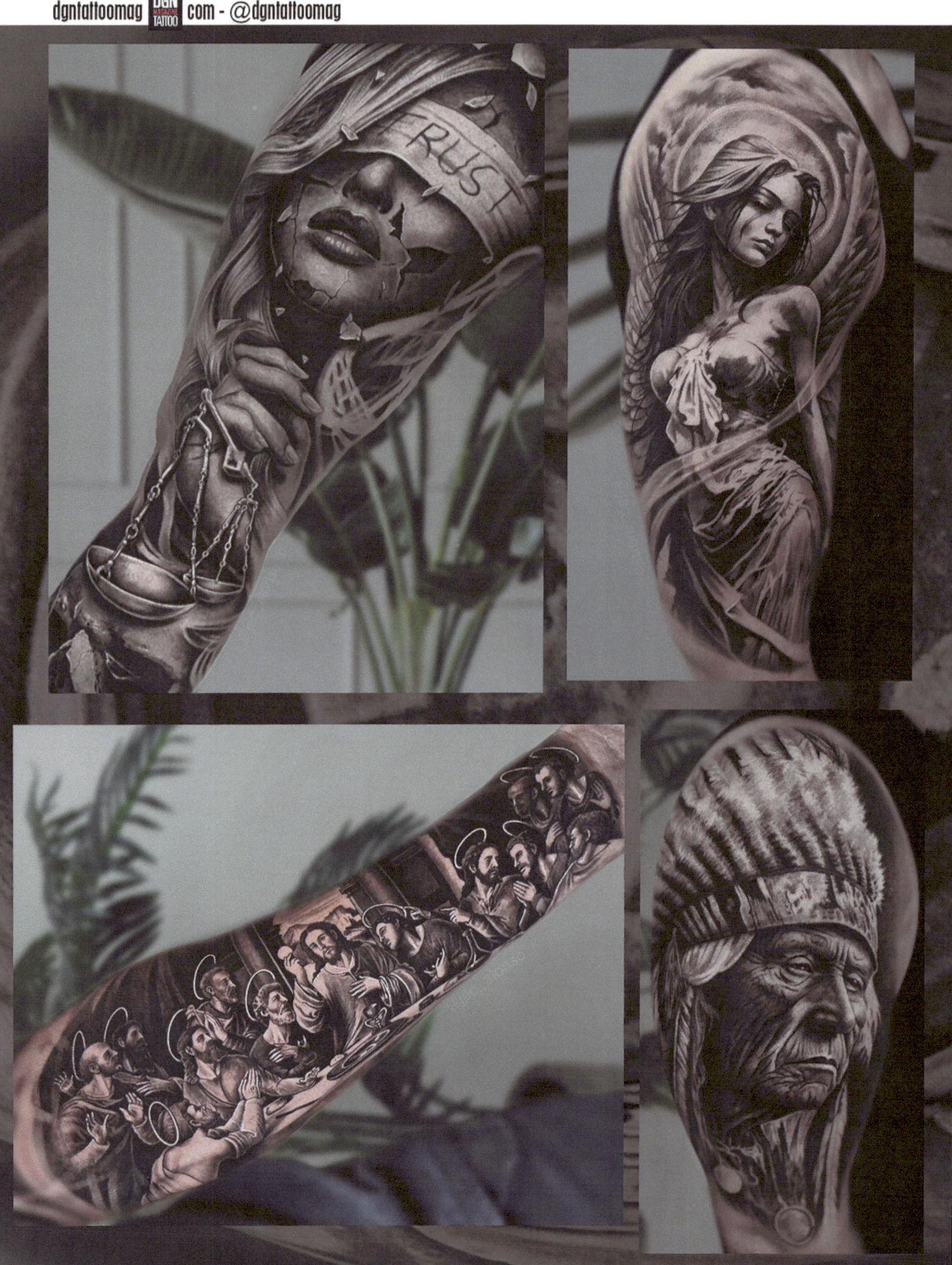

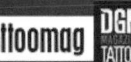

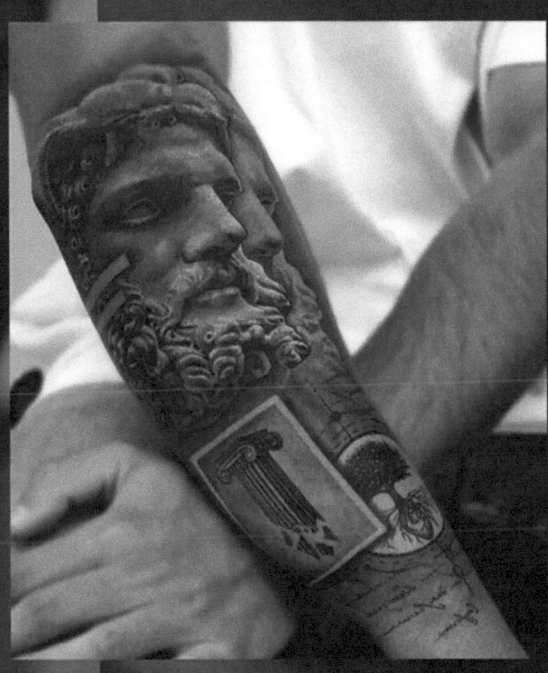

8. - Do you participate in tattoo conventions or events related to tattooing?

8. Yes, this year I have the honor of attending the Empire State Tattoo Convention in Manhattan, New York. Additionally, I'll be part of the jury at another convention in Connecticut. These events are incredible opportunities to connect with other artists, showcase my work, and learn about the latest trends in the tattoo industry

9. - Is there any project or professional goal you would like to achieve in the near future?

9. Yes, I have several projects and professional goals that I would like to achieve in the near future. One of them is to continue expanding my presence in the tattoo industry, both nationally and internationally. Additionally, I'd like to explore new techniques and styles in my work, as well as collaborate with other prominent artists. I also aim to participate in more tattoo conventions and related events to continue growing and learning in this exciting world of body art.

10. - How is your year going so far?

10. So far, my year has been exciting and full of learning. Both personally and professionally, I've experienced significant growth. Bringing my family from Spain to the United States to embark on this

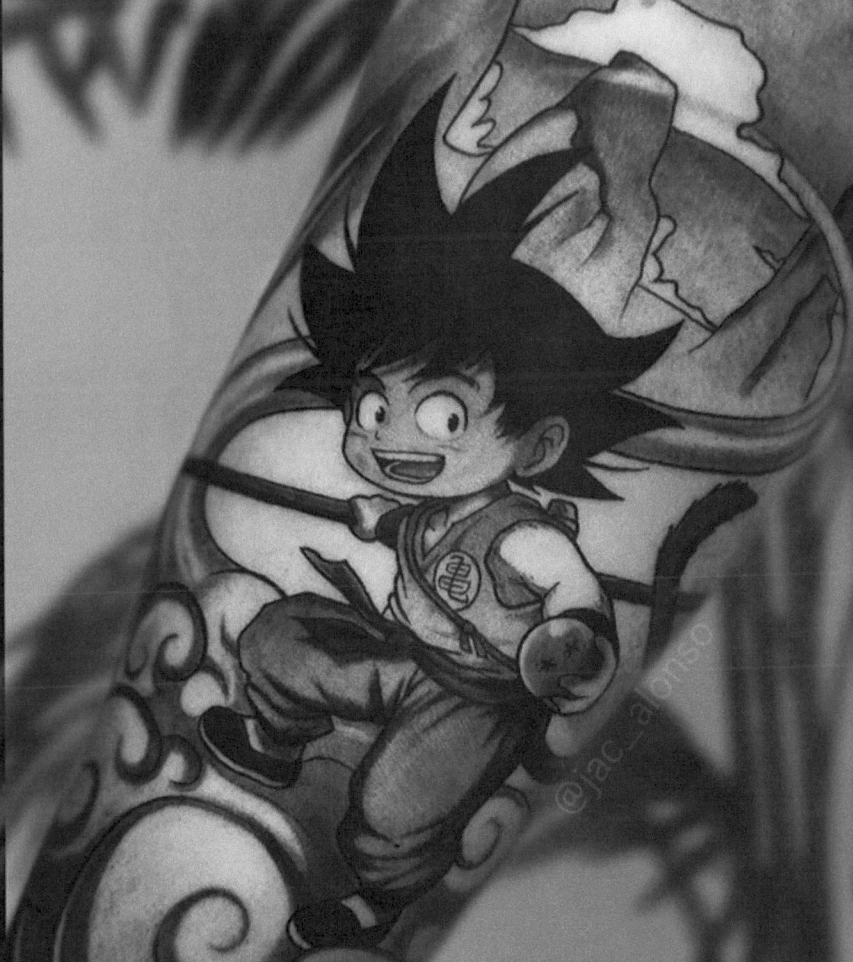

@jac_alonso

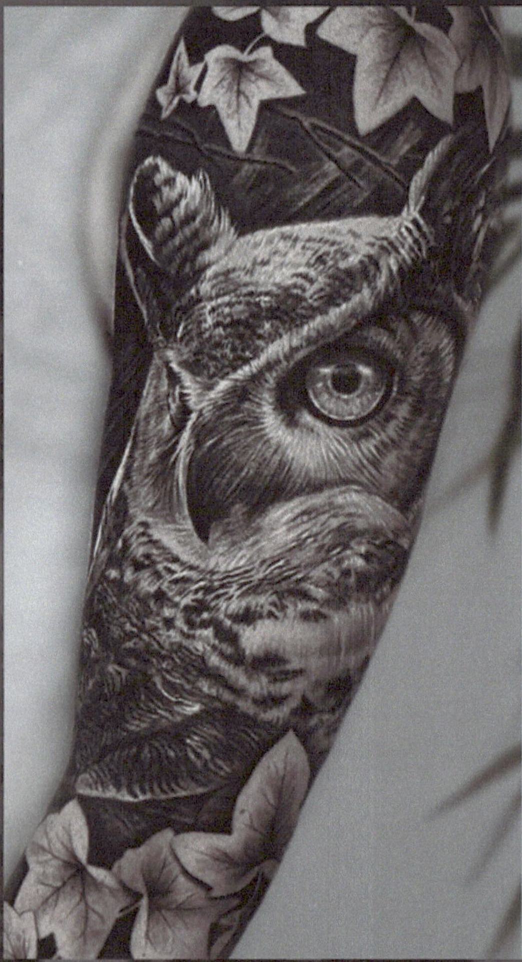

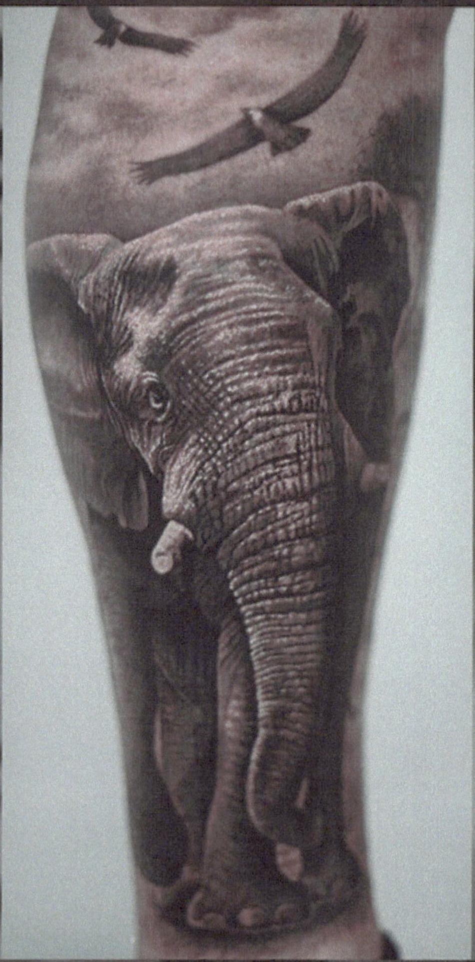

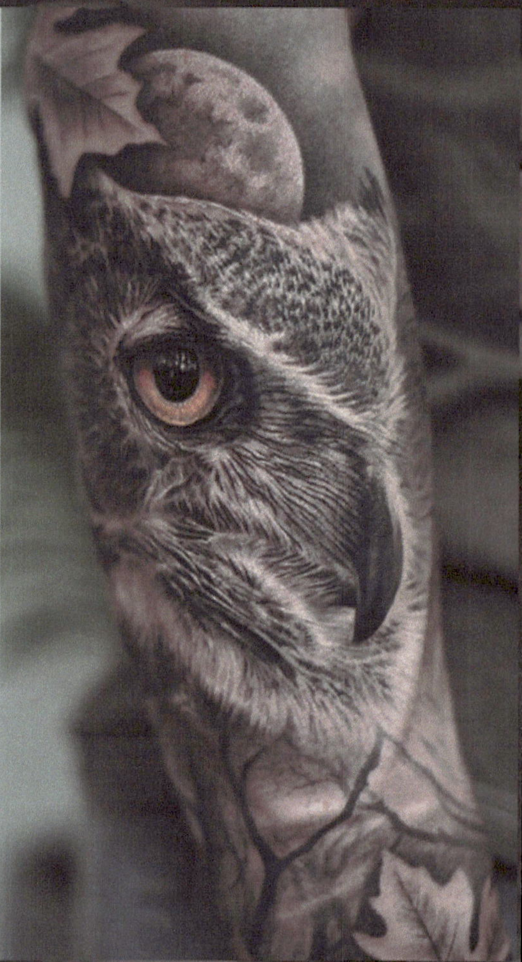

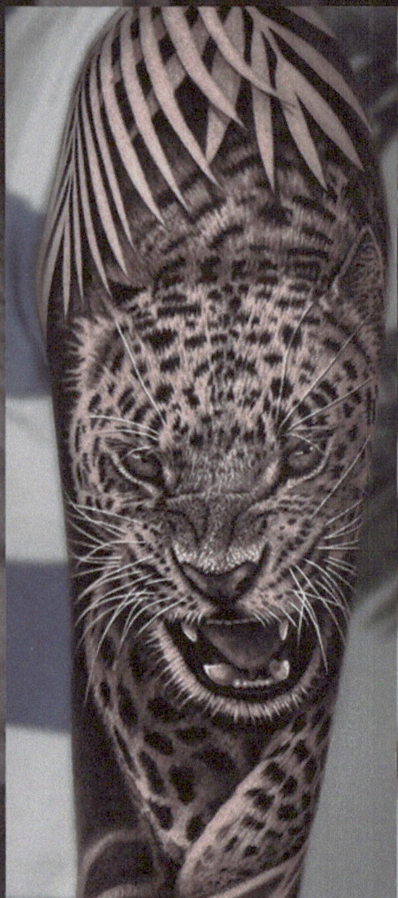

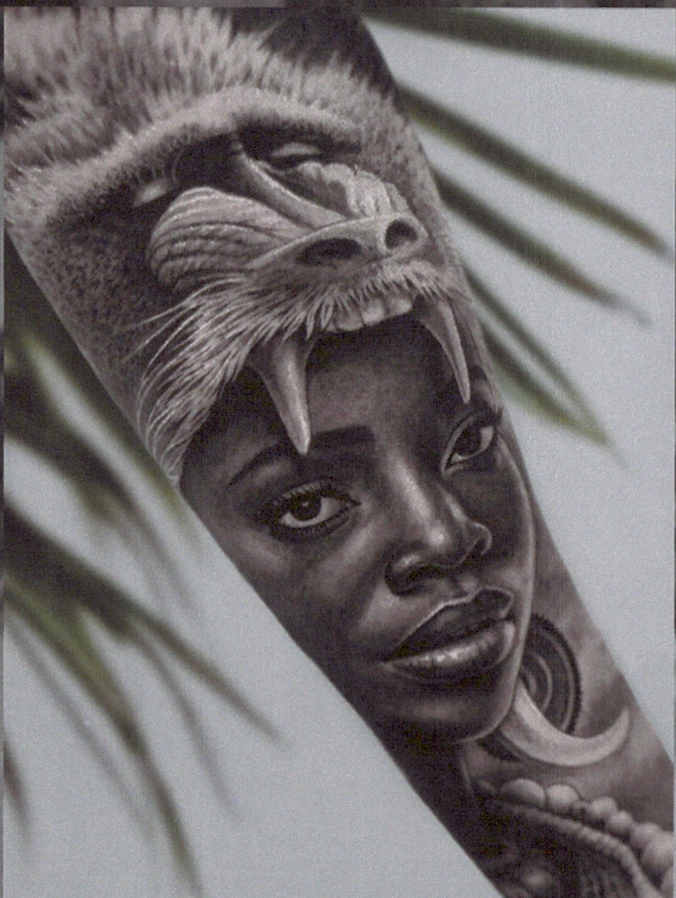

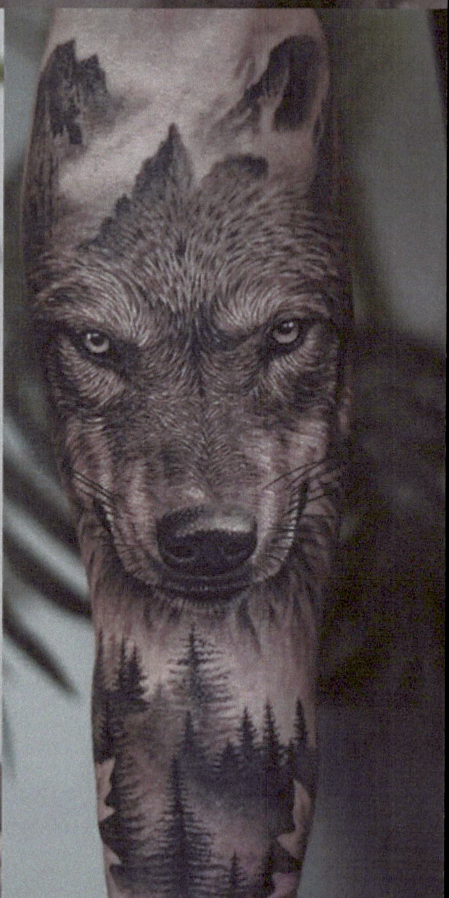

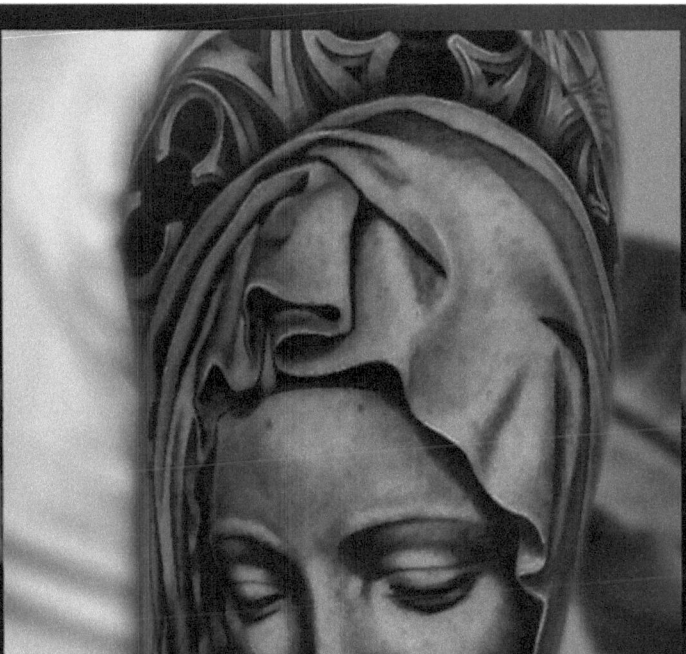

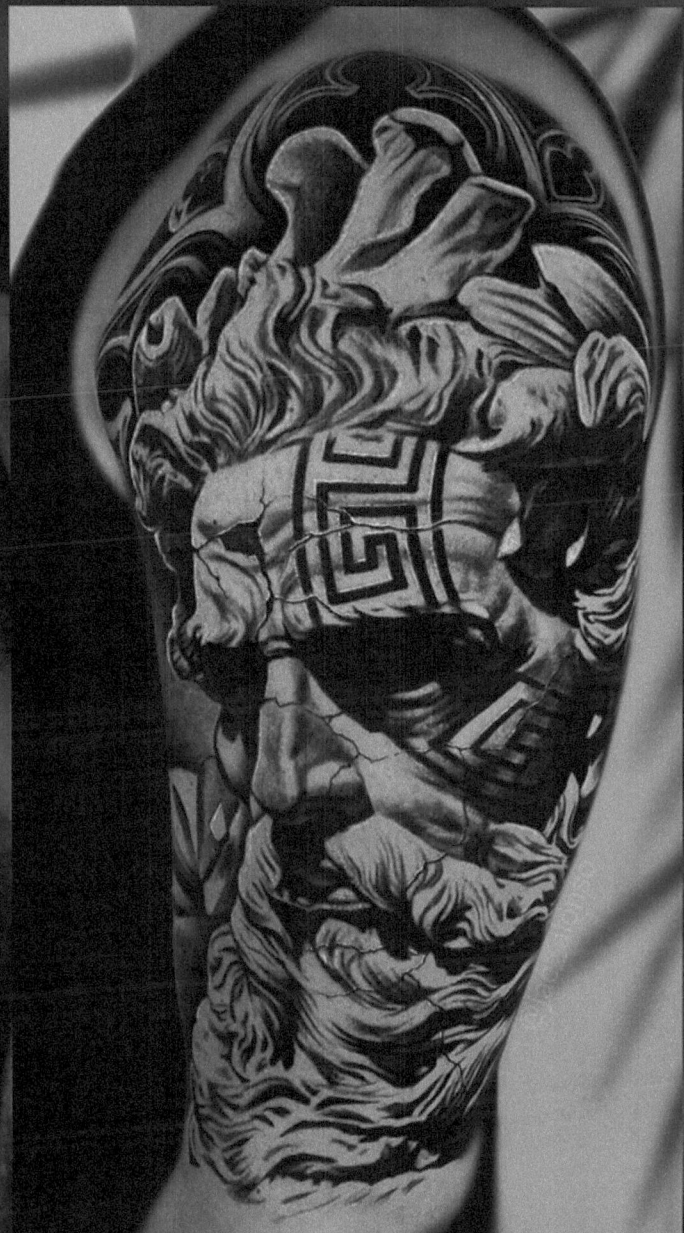

adventure together has been a truly enriching experience. In my career as a tattoo artist, I've been exploring new techniques and styles, allowing me to expand my skills and creativity. Additionally, participating in events and conventions has provided me with the opportunity to connect with other artists and continue my development in this fascinating world of tattooing. I'm excited for what the future holds and eager to continue growing throughout the year.

11. - Acknowledgements...

11. I would like to take this opportunity to express my heartfelt gratitude to my family and friends for their unwavering support in this decision to move to New York. I also want to extend a special thank you to my wife for her invaluable support and courage during this transition, and to my children for their incredible adaptability. To Matías Noble, my deepest thanks for your generous support, wise critiques, and valuable advice, which have been instrumental in improving and refining my tattooing technique. Noble Art Studio in Manhattan truly feels like home to me, and I am endlessly grateful for the opportunity to work alongside you and the entire team. Additionally, I want to express my gratitude to all my clients who trust in my work. Without their support and trust, I would not have come this far in my career. Thank you to everyone for being part of this incredible journey with me!

SYDNEY / AUSTRALIA
Originally from south KOREA @Ginger_Jeong, Ginger_Blk

GINGER
JEONG

Ginger Jeong, a tattoo artist originally from South Korea who is now making waves in Sydney, Australia. His style is a unique blend of fine line American traditional with captivating Asian influences. Jeong's journey into tattooing began in an unexpected way , but despite lacking formal art training, he pursued his passion with determination, learning from mentors and immersing himself in self-study. His work reflects a beautiful fusion of cultures, drawing from his Korean heritage and his global travels.

1. How would you describe your style? What elements distinguish it from other styles?

It's always difficult to describe what style I do.
I actually do everything I can do but mainly do fine line style. More specifically, fine line American traditional, Asian style.

2. What inspires you when creating your tattoo designs? Are there any recurring themes or cultural influences in your work?

When I do American traditional style, I usually get inspired by other traditional artists, vintage flashes, paintings, books and posters as well.
And for Asian style, I want them to have a sort of traditional Korean look but that's not too

easy because there's not many references, photos and ideas. So I visited Korea recently and went to temples, museums and galleries to get ideas how I can combine them.

3. How do you define the relationship between your culture and your tattoo art? Are there aspects of your heritage reflected in your designs?

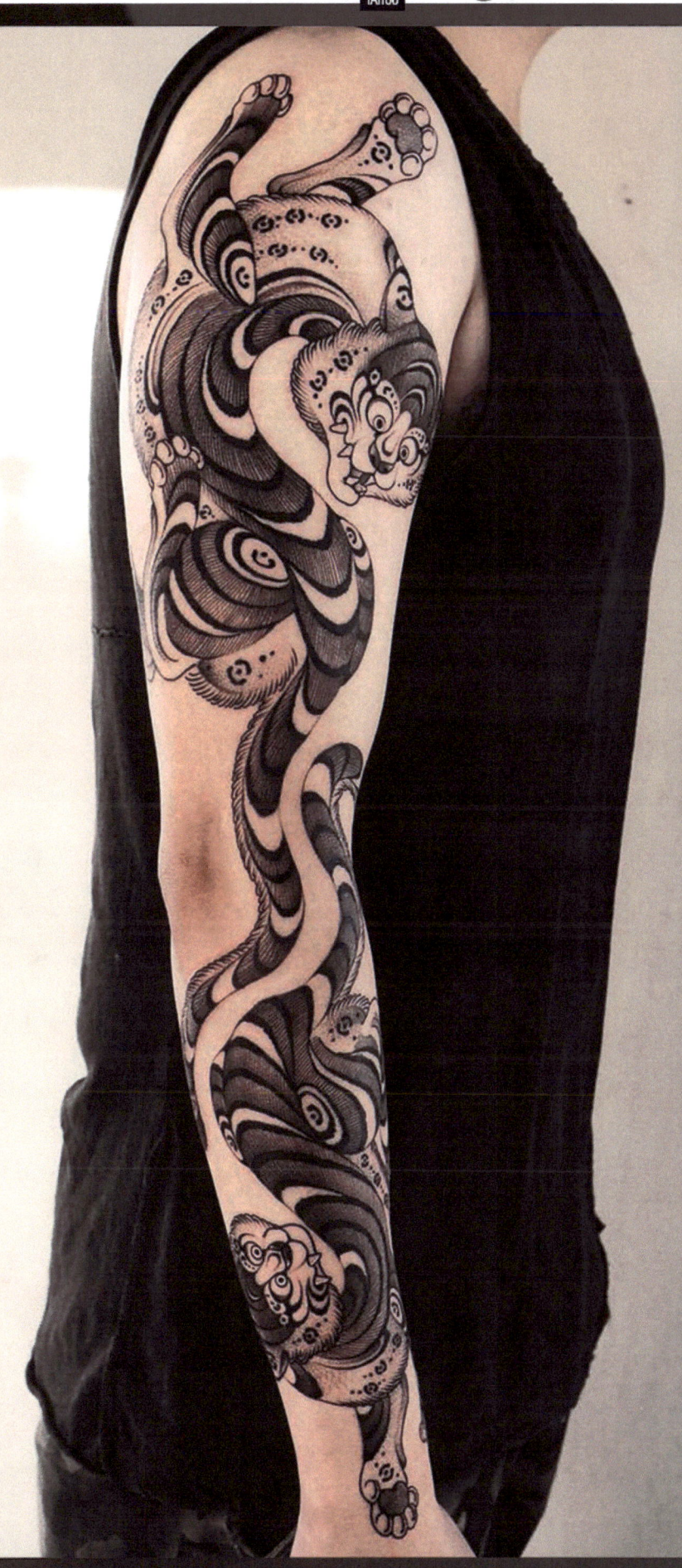

Tattoo culture in Korea is not long. I wouldn't say my tattoo art is from 'Korean tattoo culture'but still have some things that I can get inspired by like old Korean tiger paintings, traditional architectural style and stuff. You can see a kind of old Korean style painting looking at my Korean tigers.

4. How did you get started?

When I was younger, a friend of mine who I worked with got a tattoo and showed me it. It caught my eyes and I got a small tattoo after, that made me interested in tattooing. I wasn't really into art and stuff since I was very young and even had no idea how to draw a small heart. So I need a mentor and I got one. It seemed like it was going to go well but it didn't. I ended up studying by myself but luckily I met a couple friends who started tattooing about the same time as me and we drew and painted together. We shared all of our tricks and knowledge that we had.

5. What challenges do you face when merging traditional and contemporary elements in your tattoos?

I don't think it's a challenge. People have lots of freshly different ideas and get me doing something special. It makes me see the tattoo art with wider lenses.

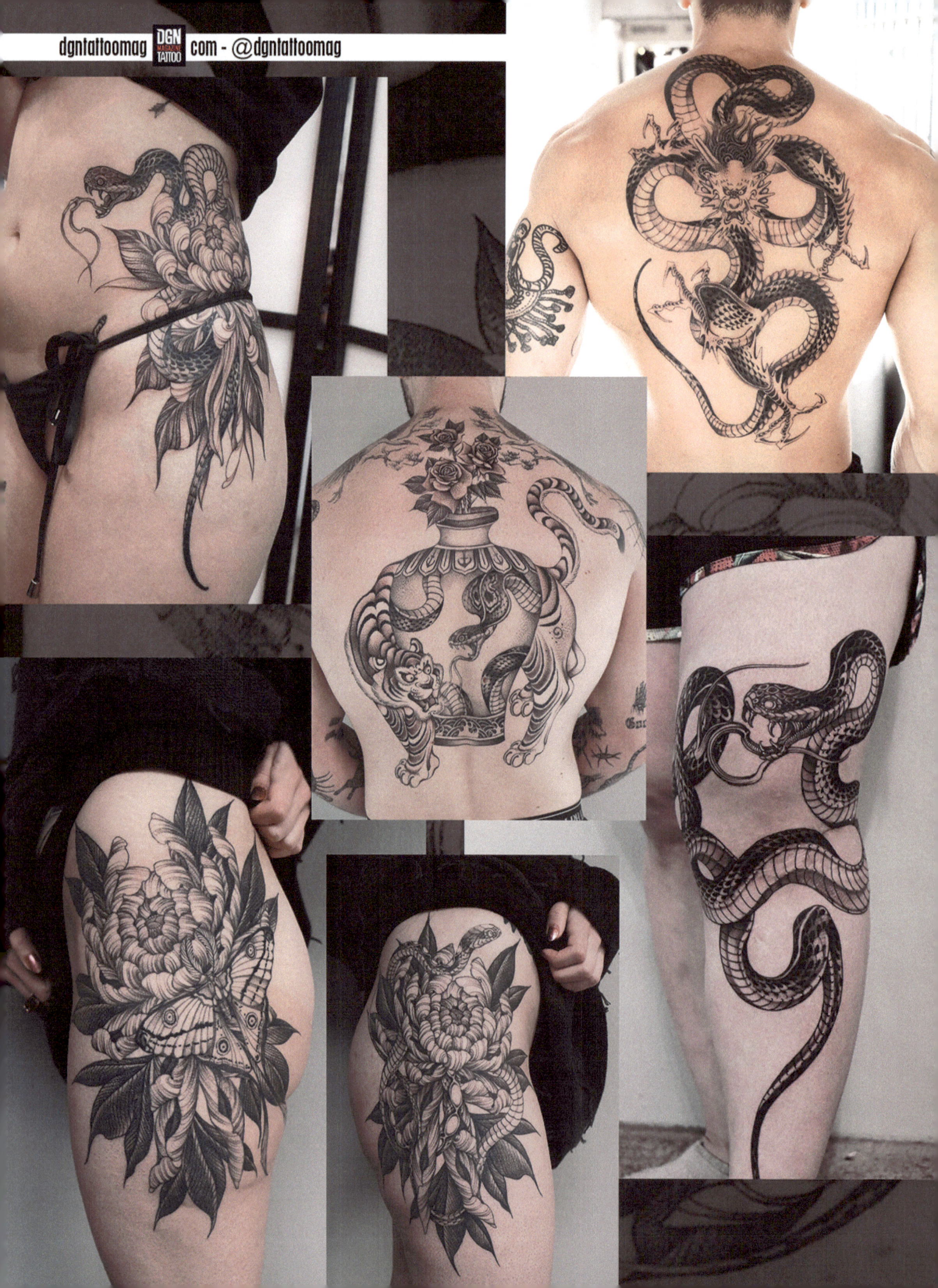

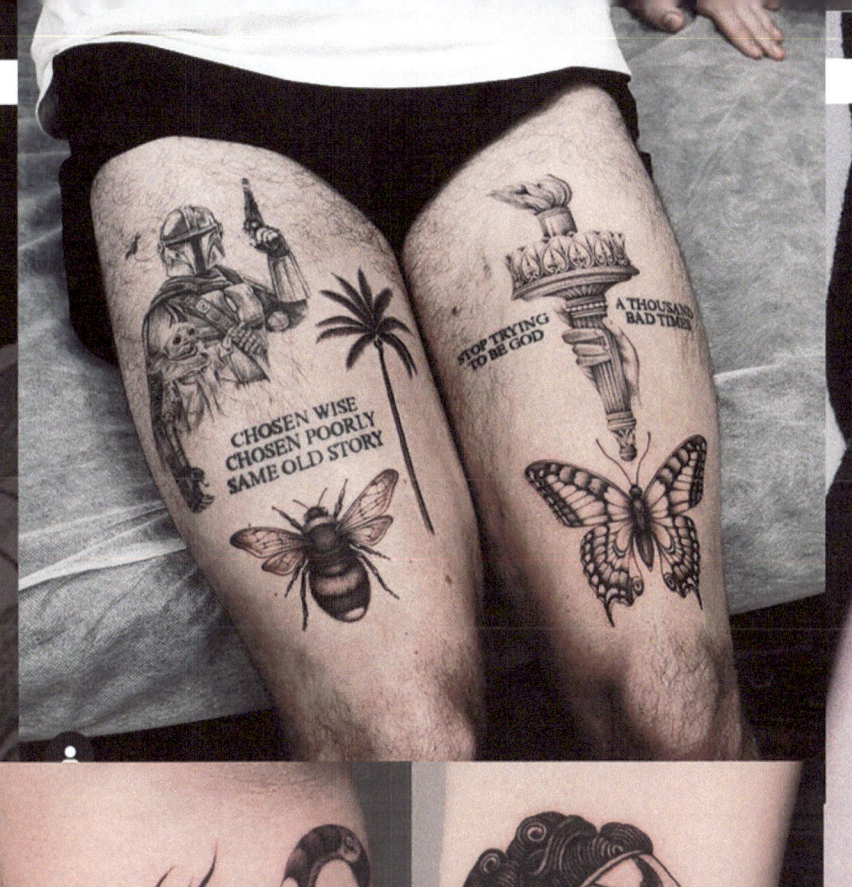

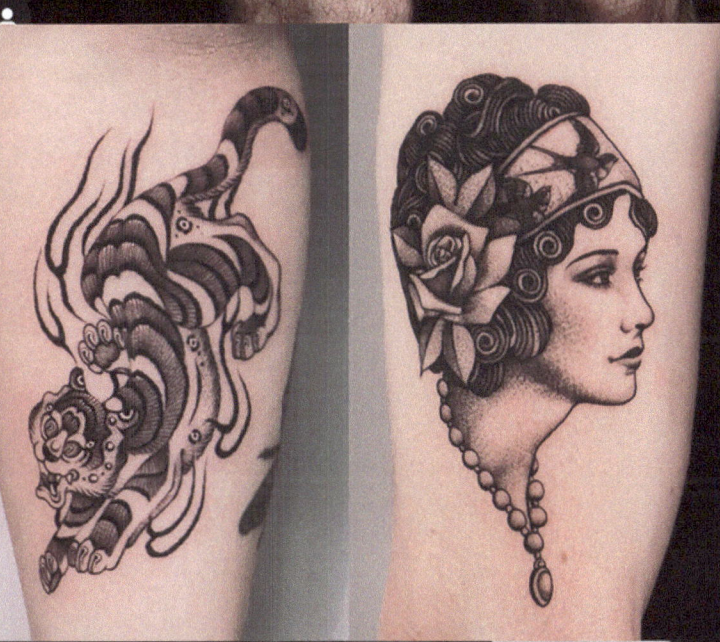

6. Could you tell us a bit about the places where you have been tattooing recently? Is there any destination that has been particularly inspiring for your work?

Past a few years I've been to a few cities. Hong Kong, Brisbane, Melbourne, Sydney and NYC. I think I usually get more inspired by who I'm with than where I am. I wanna say it's Sydney. I met so many different artists in the shop I've been working at and I learned so many things from them.

7. Do you have plans for this year?

I'd like to attend more tattoo conventions, even ones overseas and start painting too. Also want to find a way to help people with tattooing or without it.

8. We would love to know if there is anyone you would like to thank or recognize for their support in your career as a tattoo artist. Is there a mentor, colleague, or loved one who has been especially influential in your artistic journey so far?

I'd love to thank all of the people who I met in my tattooing journey.
Especially who I'm working with at The darling parlour tattoo in Sydney!

9. How can people contact you?

You can email or DM me also you can give us a call too.

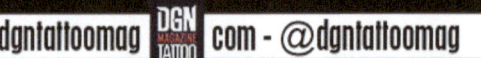
DMITRY PERUNOV

MOSCOW RUSSIA
@perunov_dmitry

Hi all. My name is Dmitry Perunov, I'm 35 years old, and I'm from Russia. I live and work in Moscow. As far back as I can remember from my childhood, I have always loved to draw. At the age of 14, I graduated from a children's art school. After that, I was involved in wood carving for a long time. At the age of 21, I suffered a work injury and lost three fingers on my right hand due to a milling machine accident. Following the accident, I had to learn to draw with my left hand, as I was originally right-handed!

Two to three years after the injury, I purchased my first basic tattoo equipment and started tattooing. Like most tattoo artists, I initially experimented with different styles, but after a few years, I transitioned entirely to black and gray realism. I particularly enjoy working with detail, creating smooth gradients, and playing with shadows.

Today, I am recognized as one of the top masters in Russia specializing in black and gray realism. I have achieved multiple victories at tattoo conventions. In my free time, I enjoy listening to heavy music and traveling; it motivates me to continue developing and not to remain stagnant.

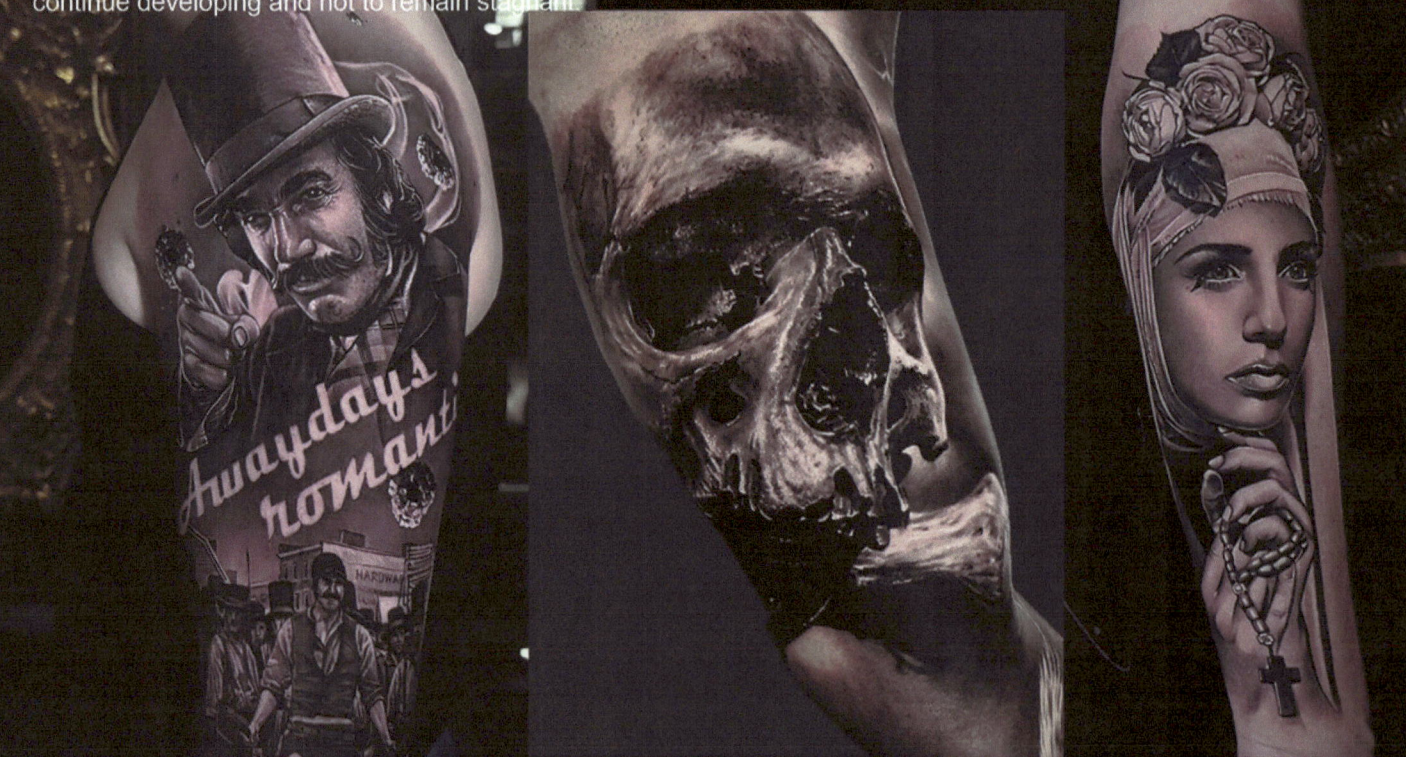

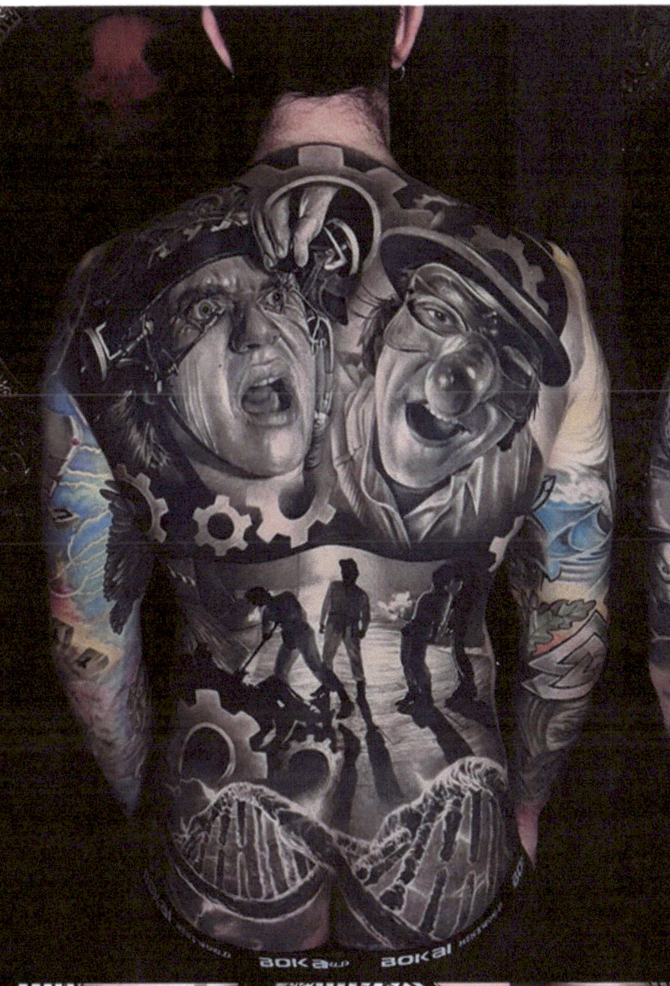

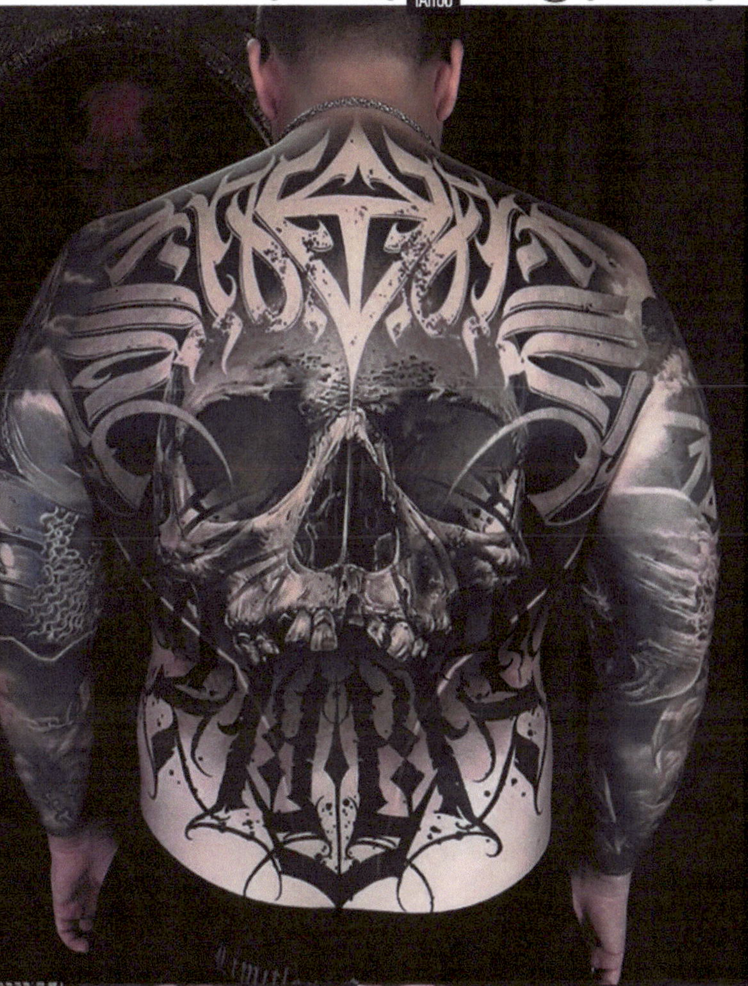

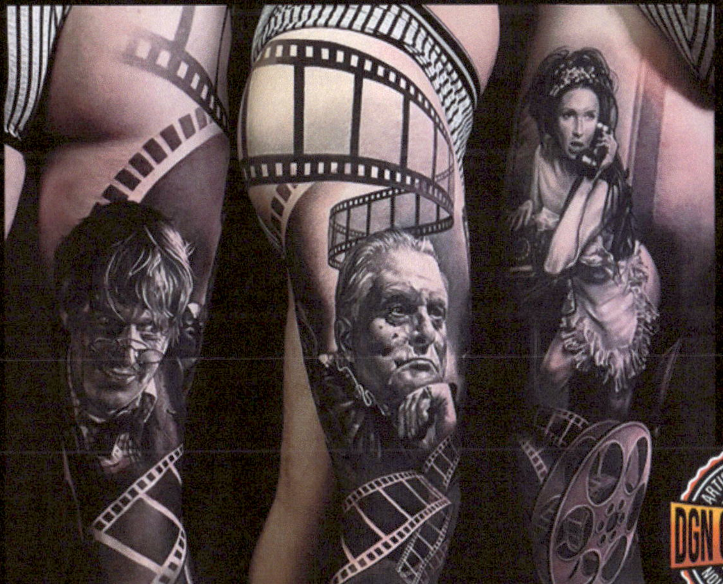

dgntattoomag 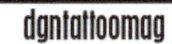 com - @dgntattoomag

DGN TATTOO MAGAZINE ®   MONTHLY EDITION - 20 YEARS - SOCIAL NETWORKS @DGNTATTOOMAG 🅾 🅵   WWW.DGNTATTOOMAG.COM

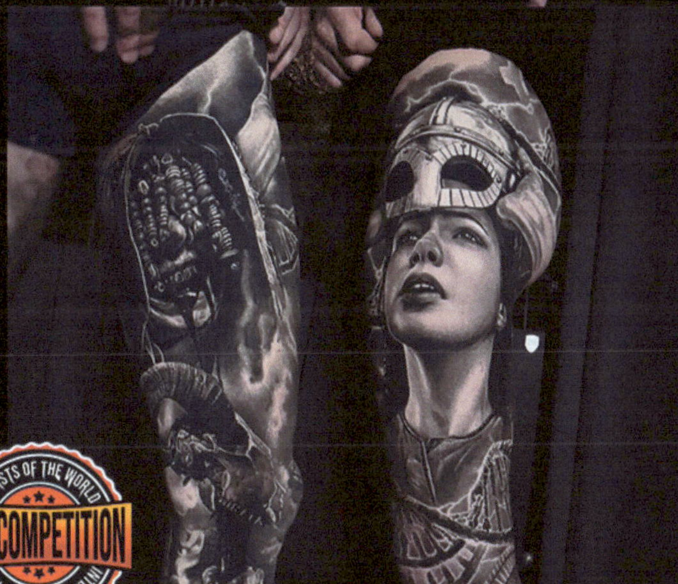

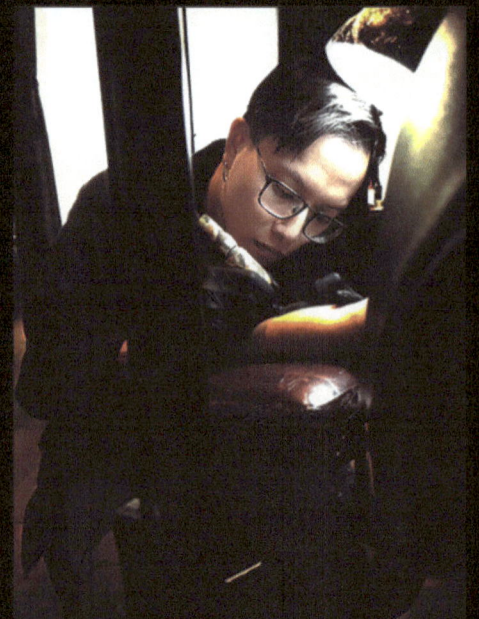

LONG DINK

PARIS **@long.dink**
FRANCE longdink1@gmail.com

Long, known as Long.Dink in the tattoo community, is a passionate and dedicated tattoo artist whose journey is as intricate and vibrant as the artwork adorning his clients' skin. Born and raised in Vietnam, Long's artistic journey began at a young age, fueled by a deep appreciation for Asian art and culture. His early exposure to traditional Vietnamese and Chinese art laid the foundation for his unique style, blending traditional techniques with modern creativity.

Eager to expand his artistic horizons, Long pursued formal art education in both Vietnam and China, immersing himself in diverse artistic traditions and mastering various mediums. However, it was the art of tattooing that truly captured his heart and ignited his passion.

Long's journey took a transformative turn when he embarked on a solo adventure to Paris, the city of art and culture. Here, amidst the bustling streets and eclectic artistic community, Long found inspiration and opportunity to hone his craft. Guided by his love for blackwork and his desire to blend traditional Asian tattoo styles with contemporary influences, Long quickly made a name for himself in the Parisian tattoo scene.

Over the years, Long's dedication to his craft and his unwavering commitment to excellence have earned him recognition and acclaim among both clients and peers. His portfolio showcases a diverse range of tattoo styles, from intricate full-back pieces to delicate cover-ups, each bearing his signature blend of tradition and innovation.

Beyond his artistic prowess, Long is known for his warm demeanor and genuine connection with his clients. With each tattoo, he strives to create not just a piece of artwork, but a meaningful and personal experience for those who entrust him with their skin.

As Long continues to push the boundaries of his artistry and explore new creative avenues, he remains steadfast in his commitment to elevating the art of tattooing and sharing his passion with the world.

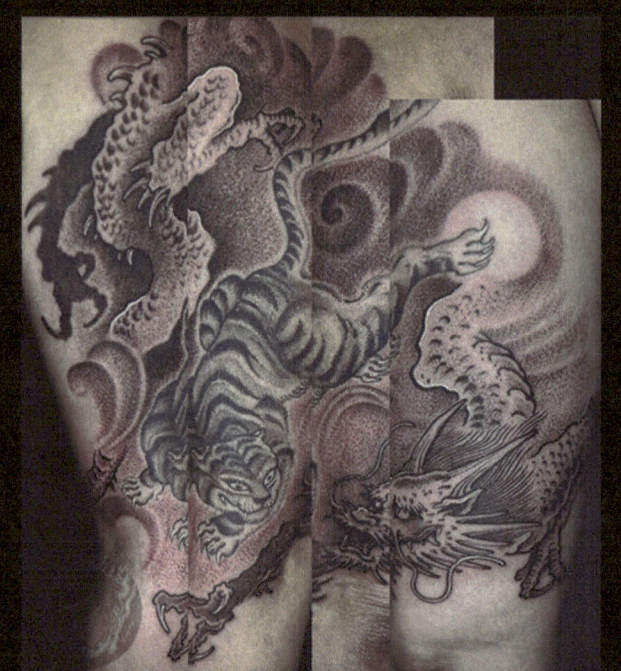

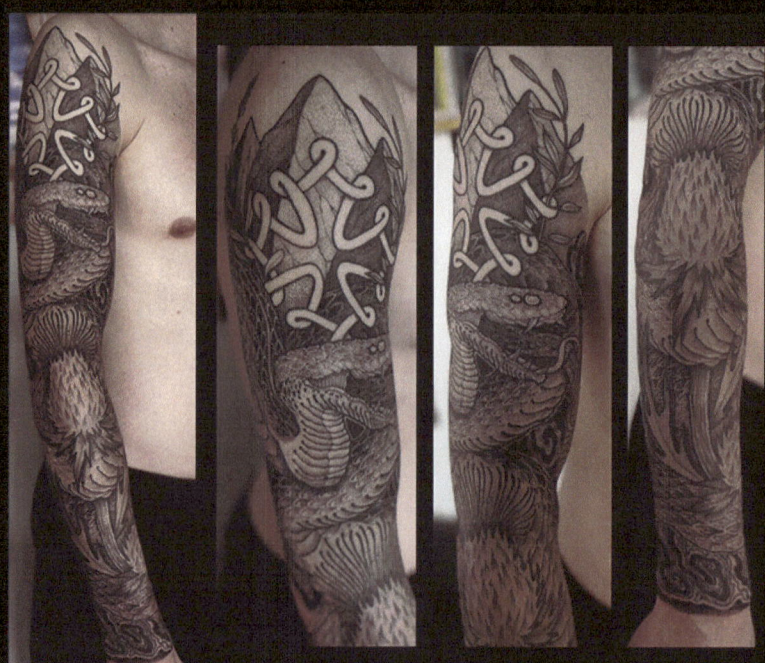

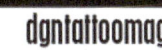

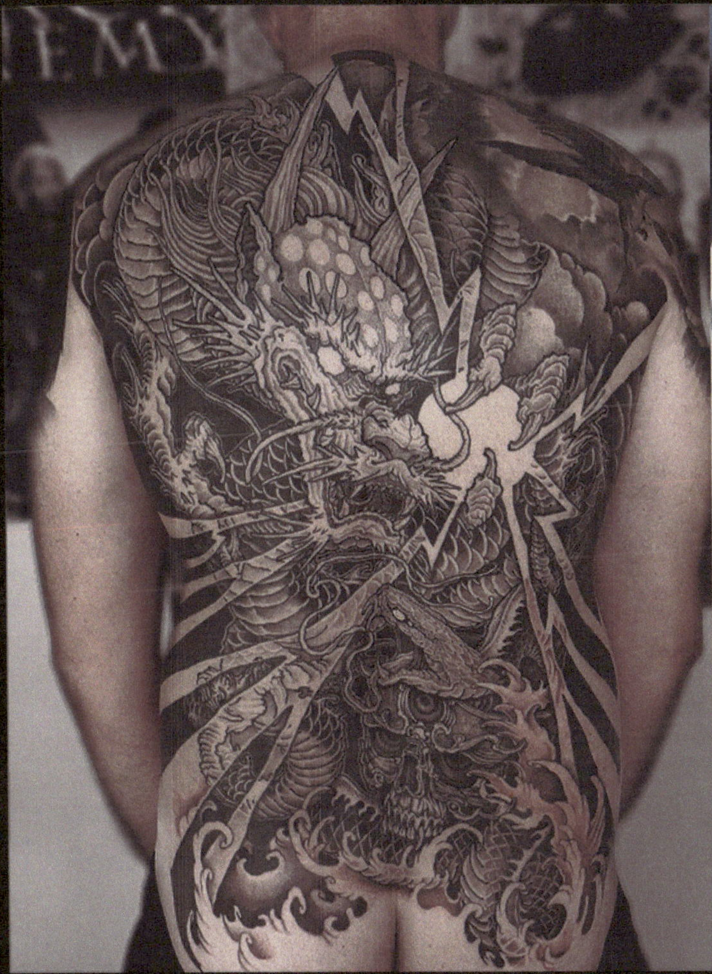

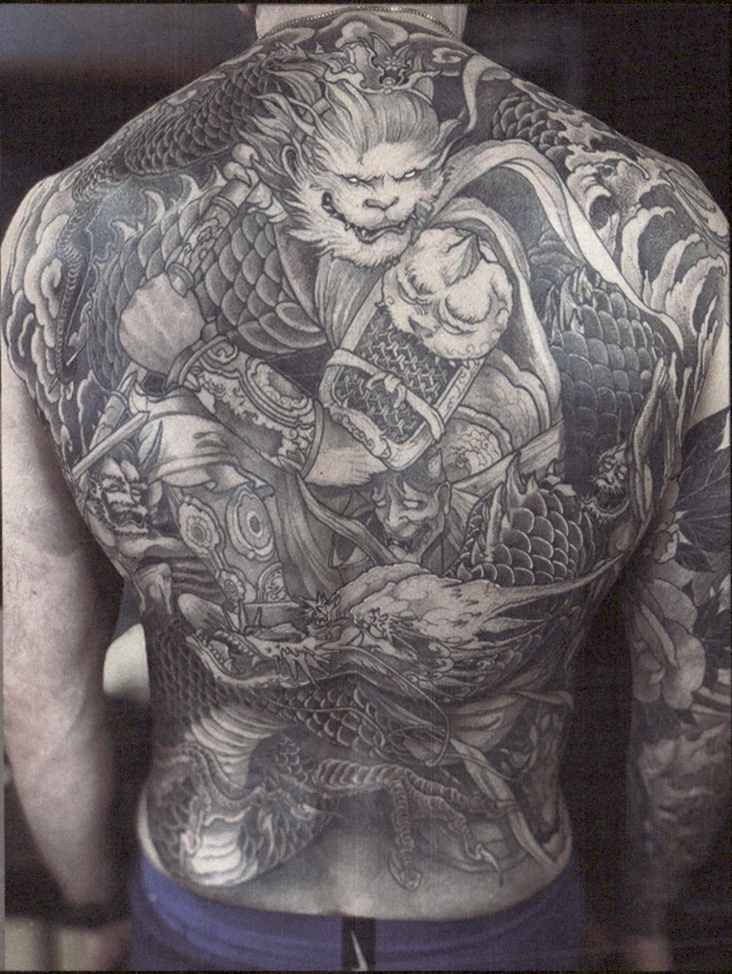

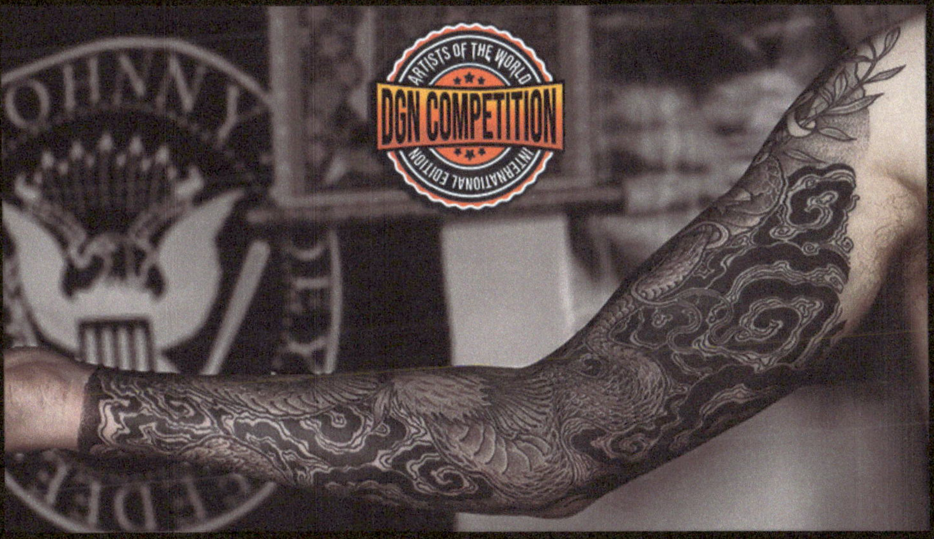

DGN COMPETITION
ARTISTS OF THE WORLD
INTERNATIONAL EDITION

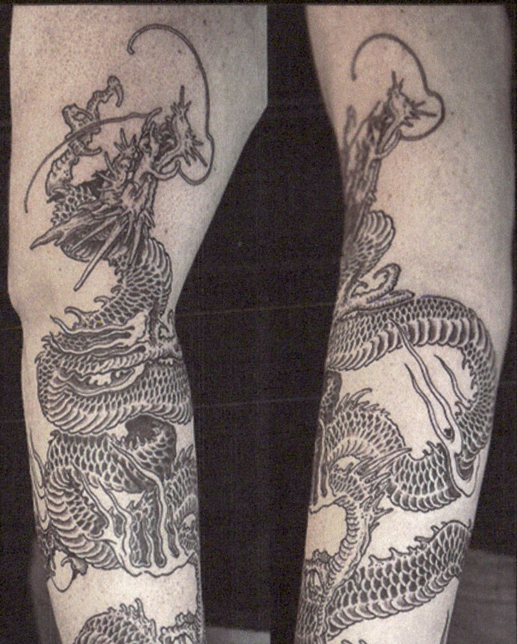

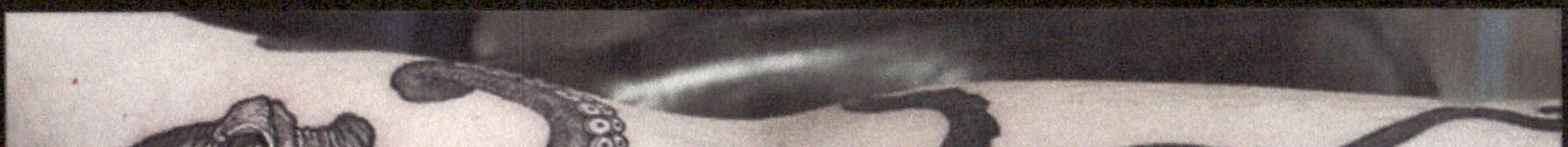

VIRGINIA PAIZ

CÓRDOBA CAPITAL ARGENTINA
@vir.paiz

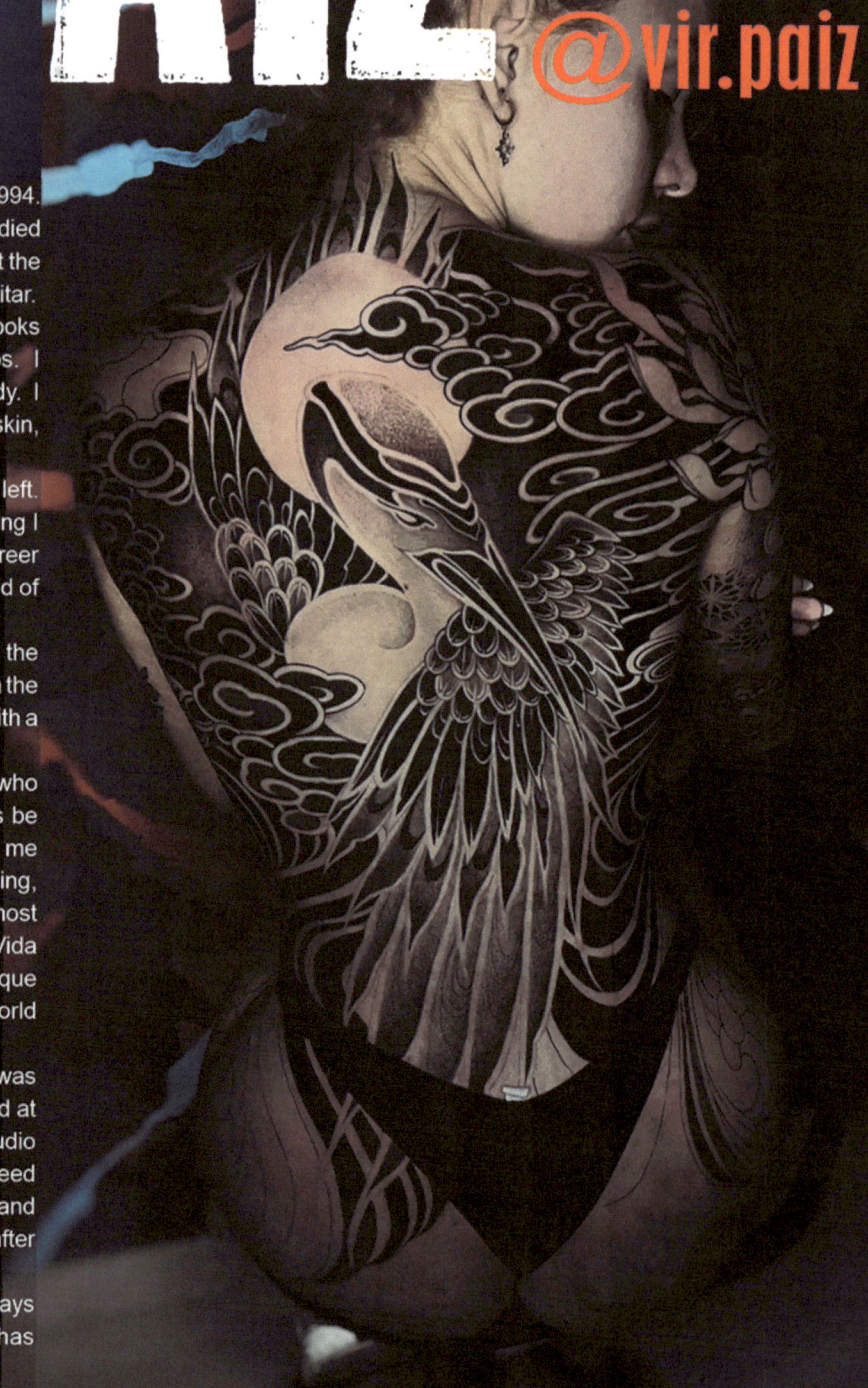

I was born in a small town in Córdoba, Argentina, in 1994. Since I was little, I felt involved with art, as my dad studied Fine Arts, so I grew up surrounded by his influence. At the age of 8, I started getting into music, specifically the guitar. My parents had a bookstore where, in addition to books and school supplies, they sold temporary tattoos. I remember being covered in them all over my body. I always had a certain fascination with art on the skin, knowing that they would be permanent in the future.

When I finished school, I pursued a career that I soon left. At the age of 19, I decided to get into music, something I was already quite familiar with. However, I left this career when I met a friend who opened the doors to the world of tattooing for me.

I got my first tattoo when I was 17. I will never forget the feeling of "this has to be my world" when I walked down the stairs of that studio. Three years later, I found myself with a machine in my hands, thus beginning my new life.

I was 20 when I did my first tattoo. I did it to the person who taught me how to tattoo, a friend whom I will always be grateful to for everything she taught me and helped me with. Three months after learning the basics of tattooing, she helped me get an apprenticeship at one of the most well-known studios of that time in the city, Buena Vida Tattoo. There, I learned not only to improve my technique but also how to deal with clients and what this new world was all about.

One of the tattoo styles I did the most in my career was geometry. I was always very neat and, above all, good at making lines. So, every person who entered the studio looking for something geometric was my guaranteed client. Over time, I tried many styles, but blackwork and geometry always came first in my style. People, after several years, sought me out specifically for this style.

I have been tattooing for 10 years and I will always continue to seek growth. Nowadays, my style has

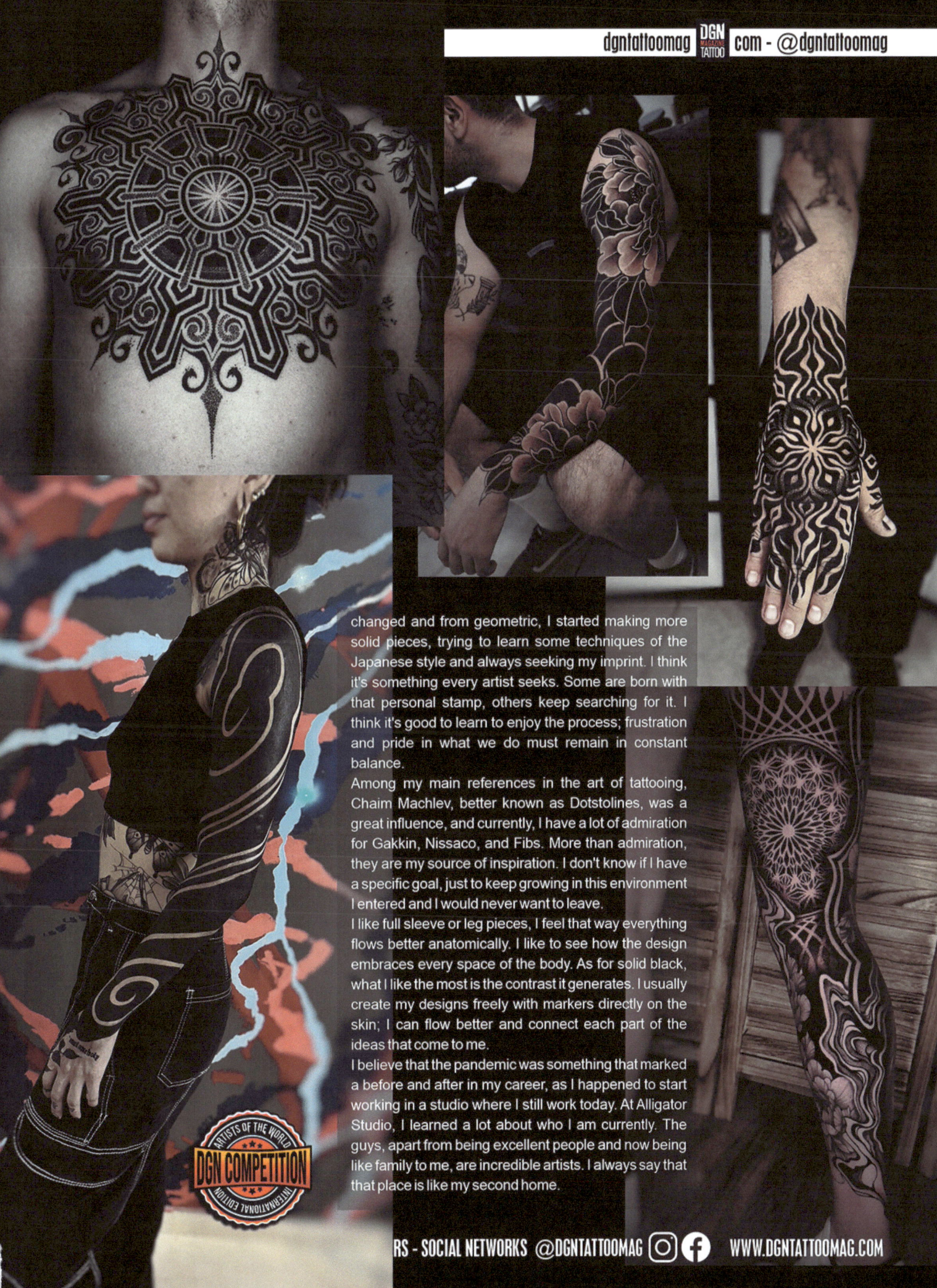

changed and from geometric, I started making more solid pieces, trying to learn some techniques of the Japanese style and always seeking my imprint. I think it's something every artist seeks. Some are born with that personal stamp, others keep searching for it. I think it's good to learn to enjoy the process; frustration and pride in what we do must remain in constant balance.

Among my main references in the art of tattooing, Chaim Machlev, better known as Dotstolines, was a great influence, and currently, I have a lot of admiration for Gakkin, Nissaco, and Fibs. More than admiration, they are my source of inspiration. I don't know if I have a specific goal, just to keep growing in this environment I entered and I would never want to leave.

I like full sleeve or leg pieces, I feel that way everything flows better anatomically. I like to see how the design embraces every space of the body. As for solid black, what I like the most is the contrast it generates. I usually create my designs freely with markers directly on the skin; I can flow better and connect each part of the ideas that come to me.

I believe that the pandemic was something that marked a before and after in my career, as I happened to start working in a studio where I still work today. At Alligator Studio, I learned a lot about who I am currently. The guys, apart from being excellent people and now being like family to me, are incredible artists. I always say that that place is like my second home.

CAMOZ ORTIZ

CALI

COLOMBIA

@camoz_tattoo
+57 3188872436

Cristhian Camilo Ortiz, known as Camoz, born in Cali, Colombia, is a 31-year-old tattoo artist passionate about visual arts since childhood. He began his journey as a tattoo artist after receiving praise for his artistic skills during a Halloween event at his former job. Although he studied electrical engineering, he decided to fully dedicate himself to the world of tattooing. Nowadays, he runs a studio in Cali, specializing in high-contrast realism and surrealism, where he enjoys transforming his clients' ideas into personalized and unique designs.

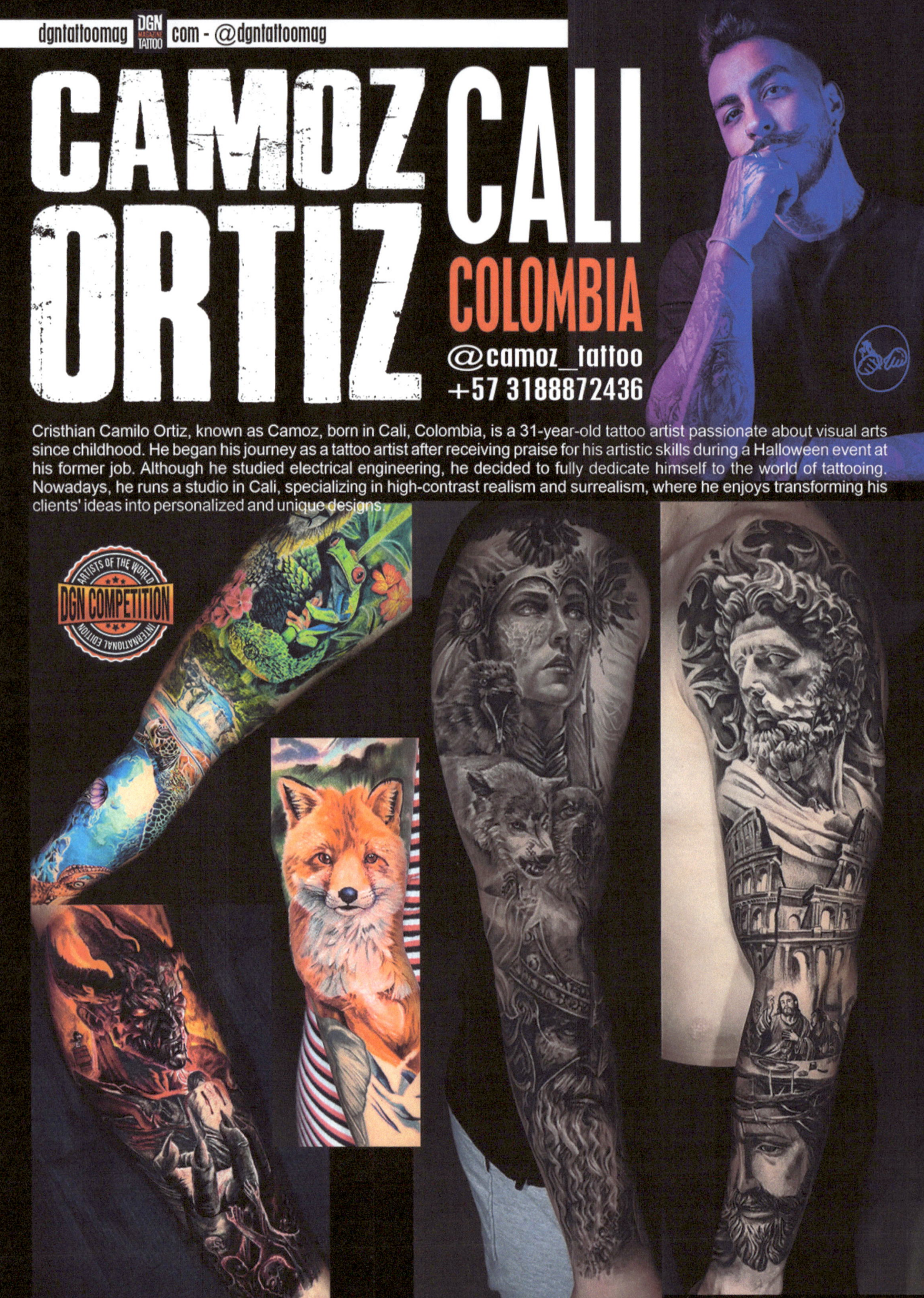

LENA
ALEKSANDROVA

KAZAN
RUSSIA
@mama.stiffera

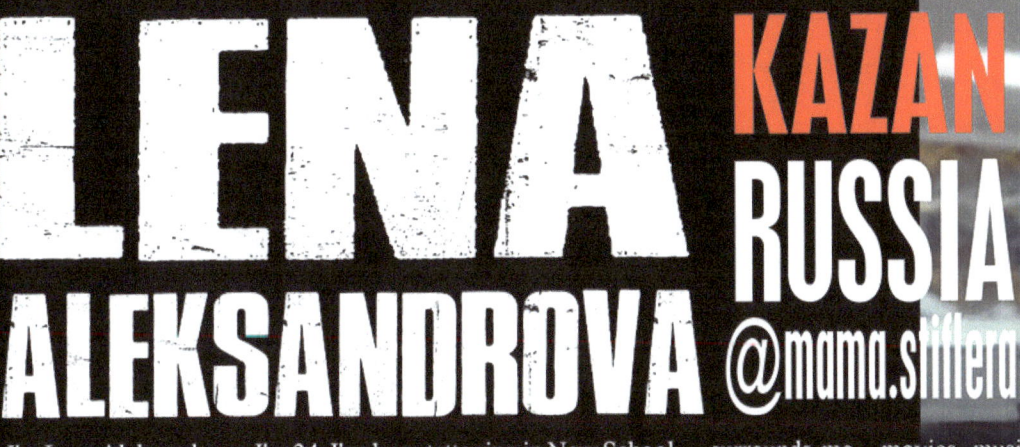

I'm Lena Aleksandrova, I'm 34. I've been tattooing in New School style for about since 2015.

Having a six-year architectural education, I still dedicated my life to tattooing. But thanks to my academic knowledge of art.

I have a few awards from Russian and German tattoo conventions. I also had the experience to participate as a judge in the Russian tattoo convention in new school category.

I make unique sketches every day, I'm inspired by everything that surrounds me - movies, music, memes, people, animals. I am excellent at stylizing characters and objects in a cartoon style. My works are distinguished by rich colors, interesting motifs, and attention to each detail.

My customers value me for my unique style, individual approach and high quality work.

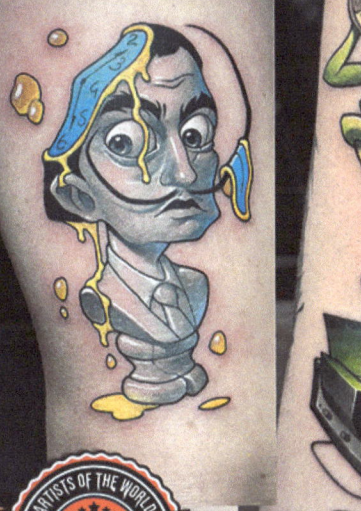

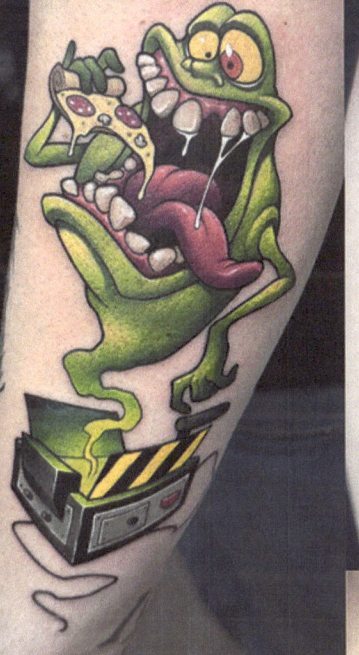

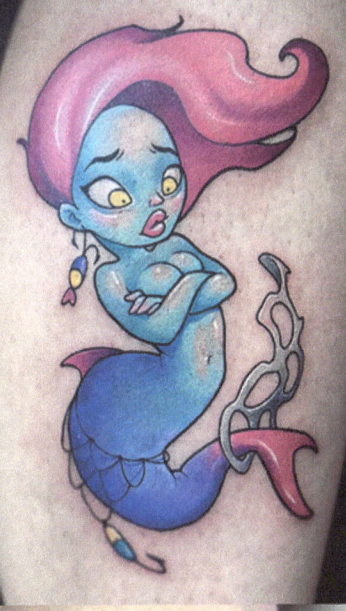

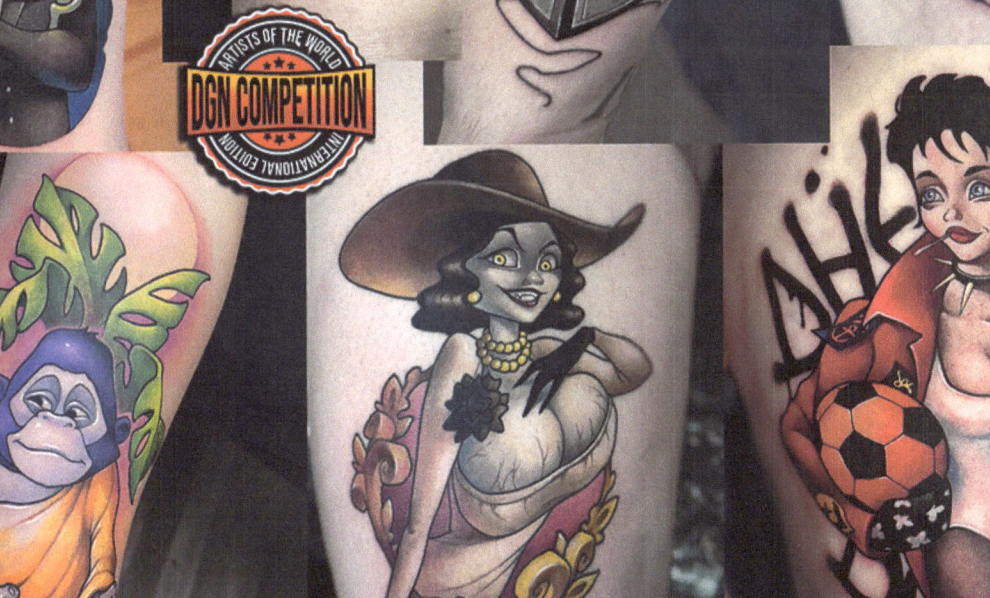

ERIK ARANGUREN

BUENOS AIRES
ARGENTINA
@tito.arte

Venezuelan tattoo artist since 2014, with 9 years in the tattoo world specializing in realism and surrealism. Additionally, he also works in styles such as new school and oriental, as these were his origins in art. Erik is a versatile artist who can execute multiple tattoo styles, as he has always been a dedicated, consistent artist willing to evolve; every step has helped him gain extensive experience and a successful career trajectory. He has won multiple awards at tattoo conventions both in Venezuela and abroad. This year, he attended the LA MILANOTATTOOCONVENTION, one of the most prestigious tattoo conventions in Europe. He currently resides in Buenos Aires, Argentina.

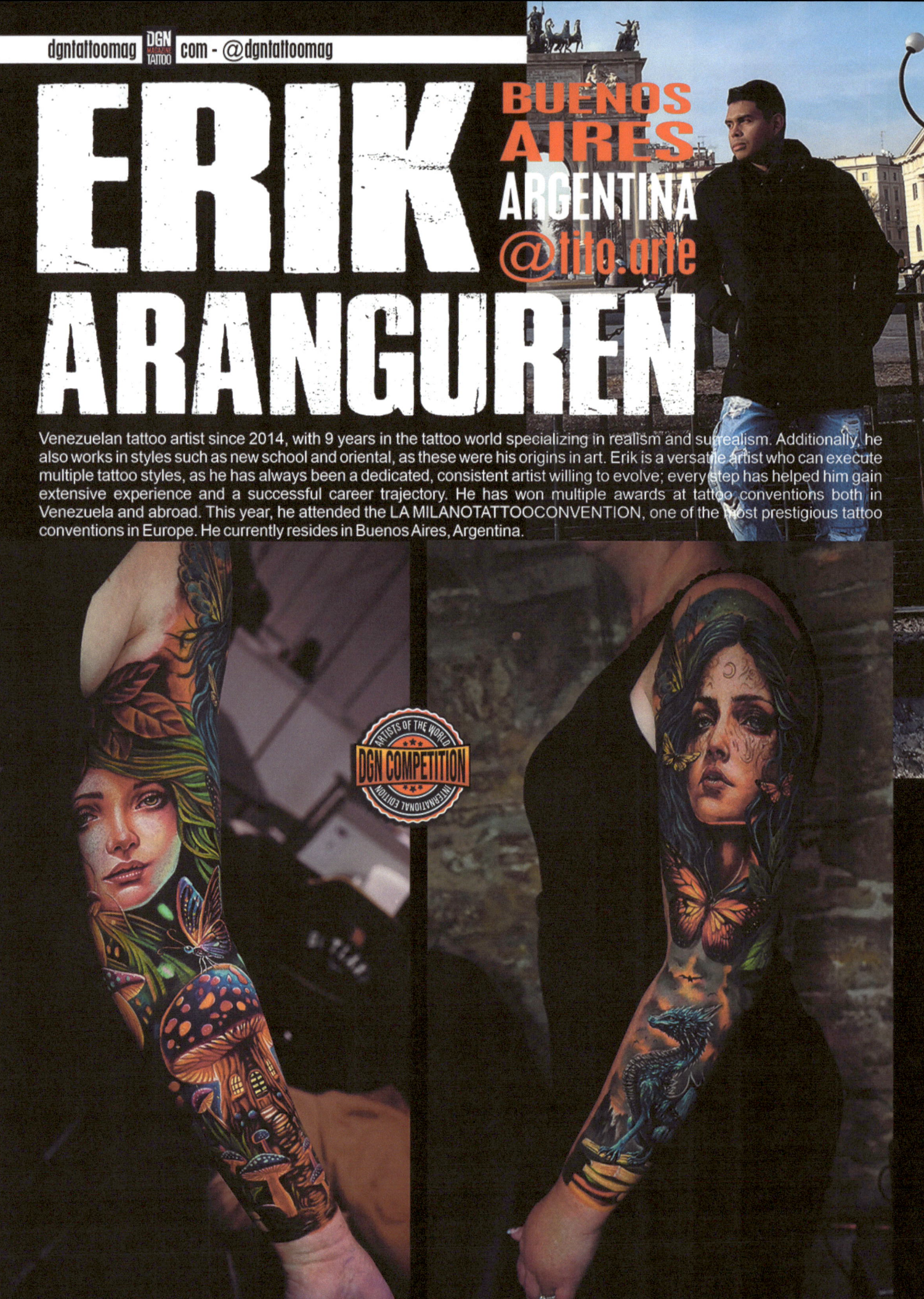

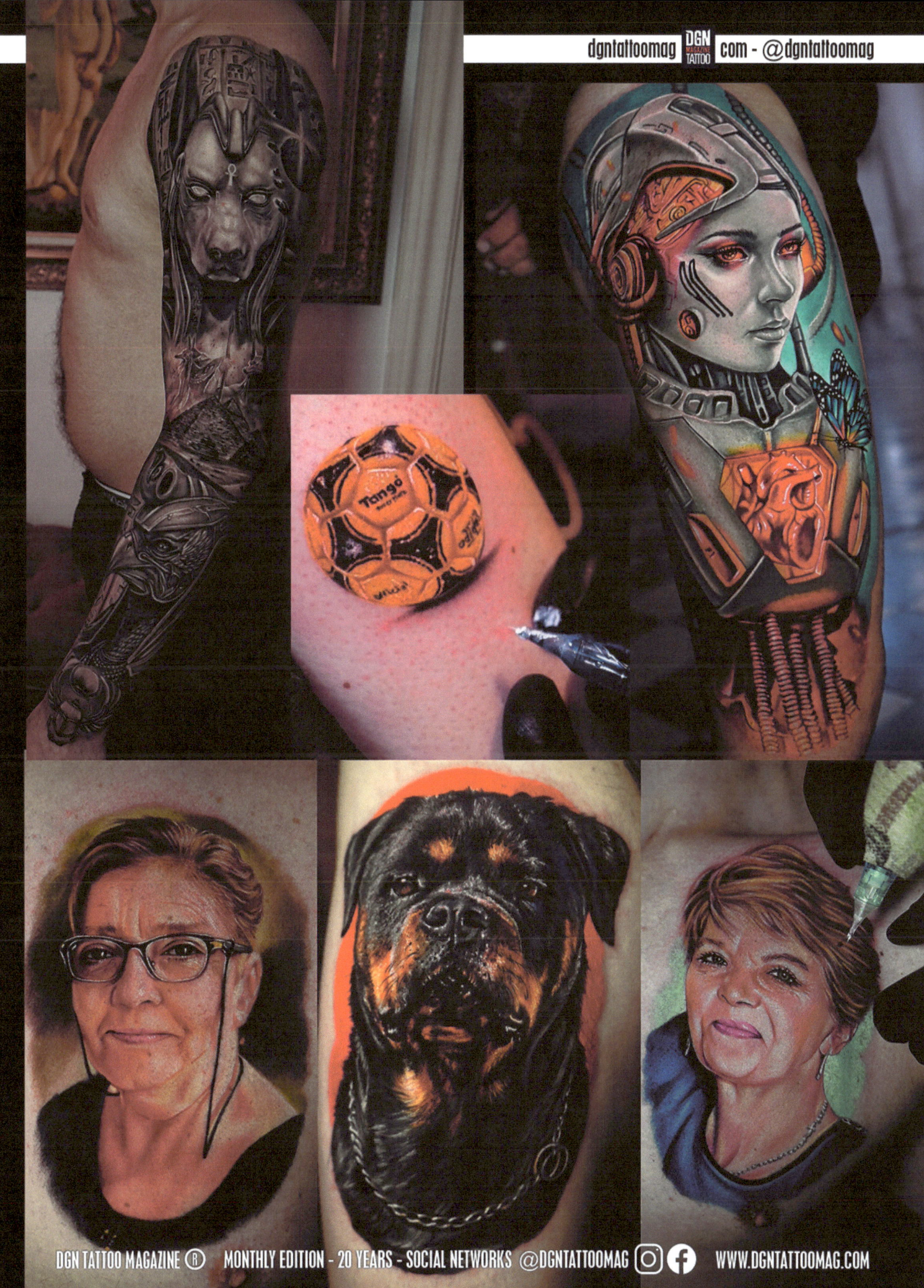

dgntattoomag **DGN** com - @dgntattoomag

DGN TATTOO MAGAZINE ® · MONTHLY EDITION - 20 YEARS - SOCIAL NETWORKS @DGNTATTOOMAG 🅾️ 🅵 WWW.DGNTATTOOMAG.COM

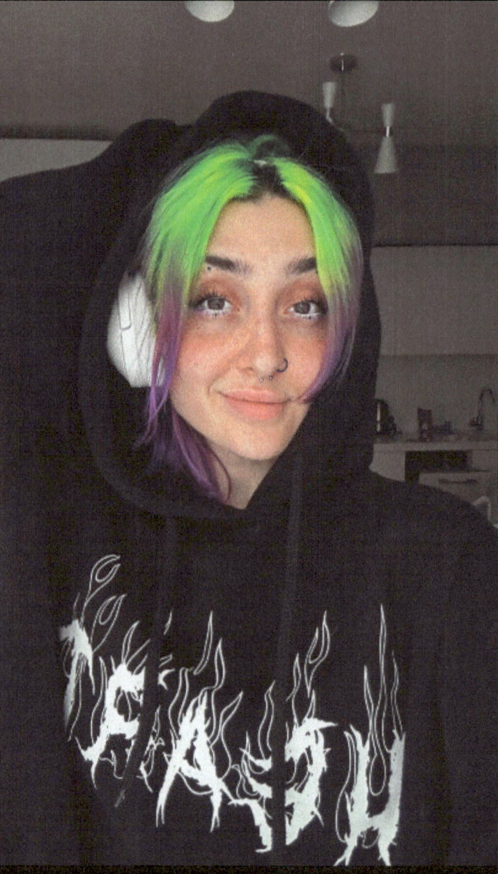

VALENTINA KOCHARIAN

ROSTOV ON DON RUSSIA

inst: @valenciaonn

Hi, my name is Valencia and I am a tattoo artist. I was born on December 11, 1997, and by the age of 26 I had come to a clear understanding that my life should be devoted to creativity. It is not the first year that I have been doing wonderful tattoos, which delight a huge number of people every day. I was born and raised in Russia, graduated from high school, university and completely went into creativity. There hasn't been a day in my life that I've regretted working in the tattoo industry. I love it because I see happy people and help them express themselves through skin art. I put a piece of myself into each of my work, so each of my work is a whole story with an interesting plot.

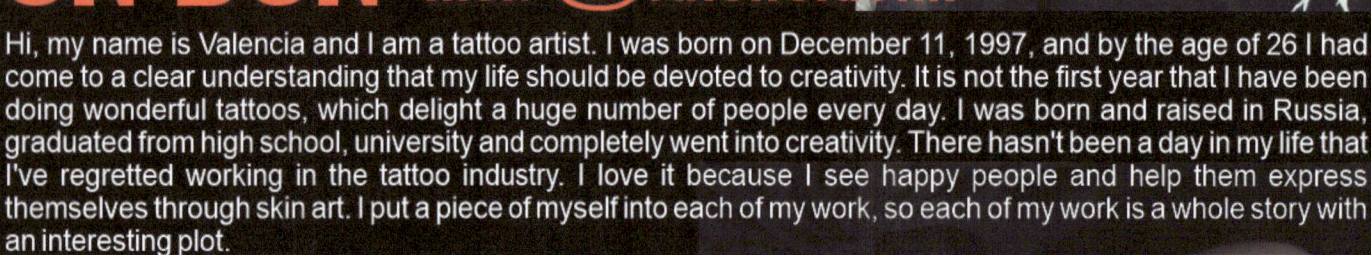

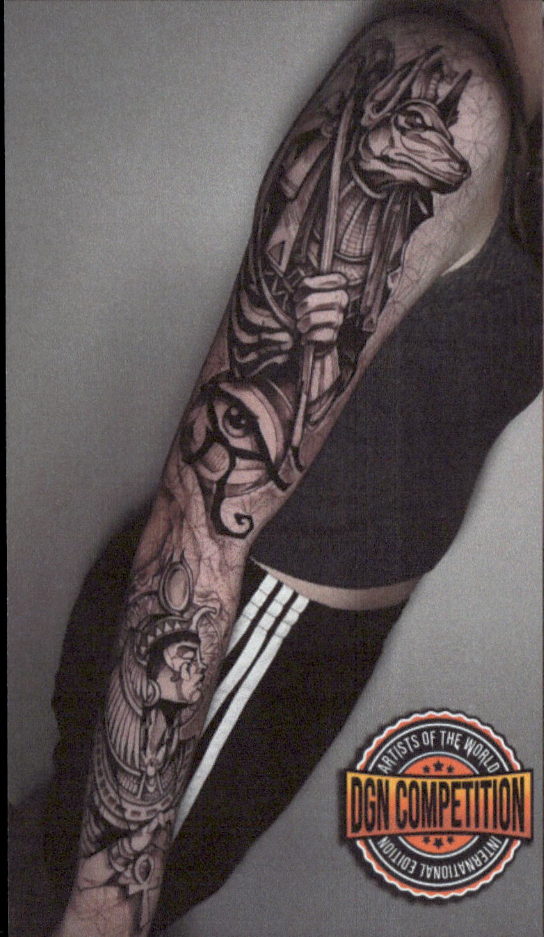

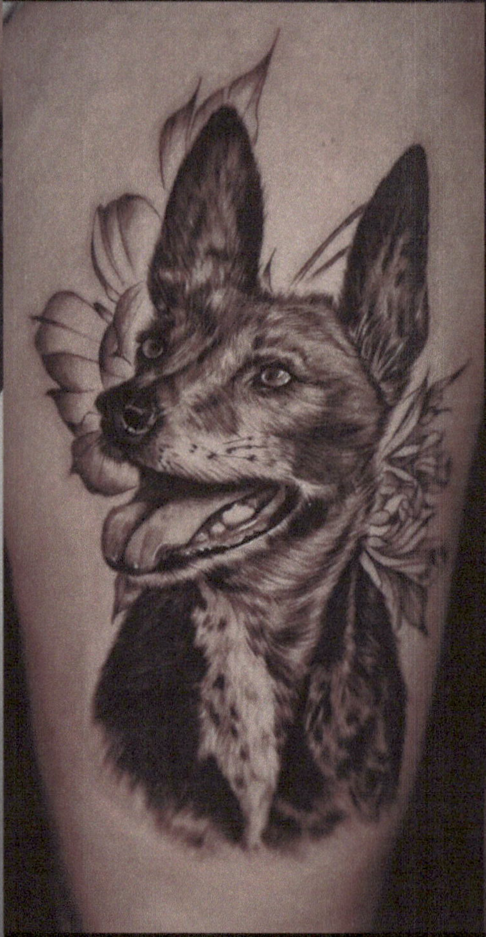

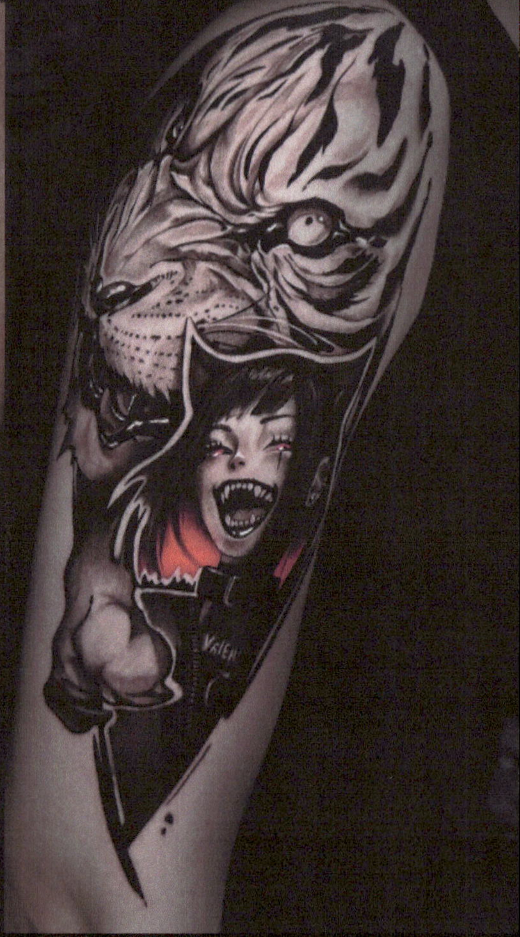

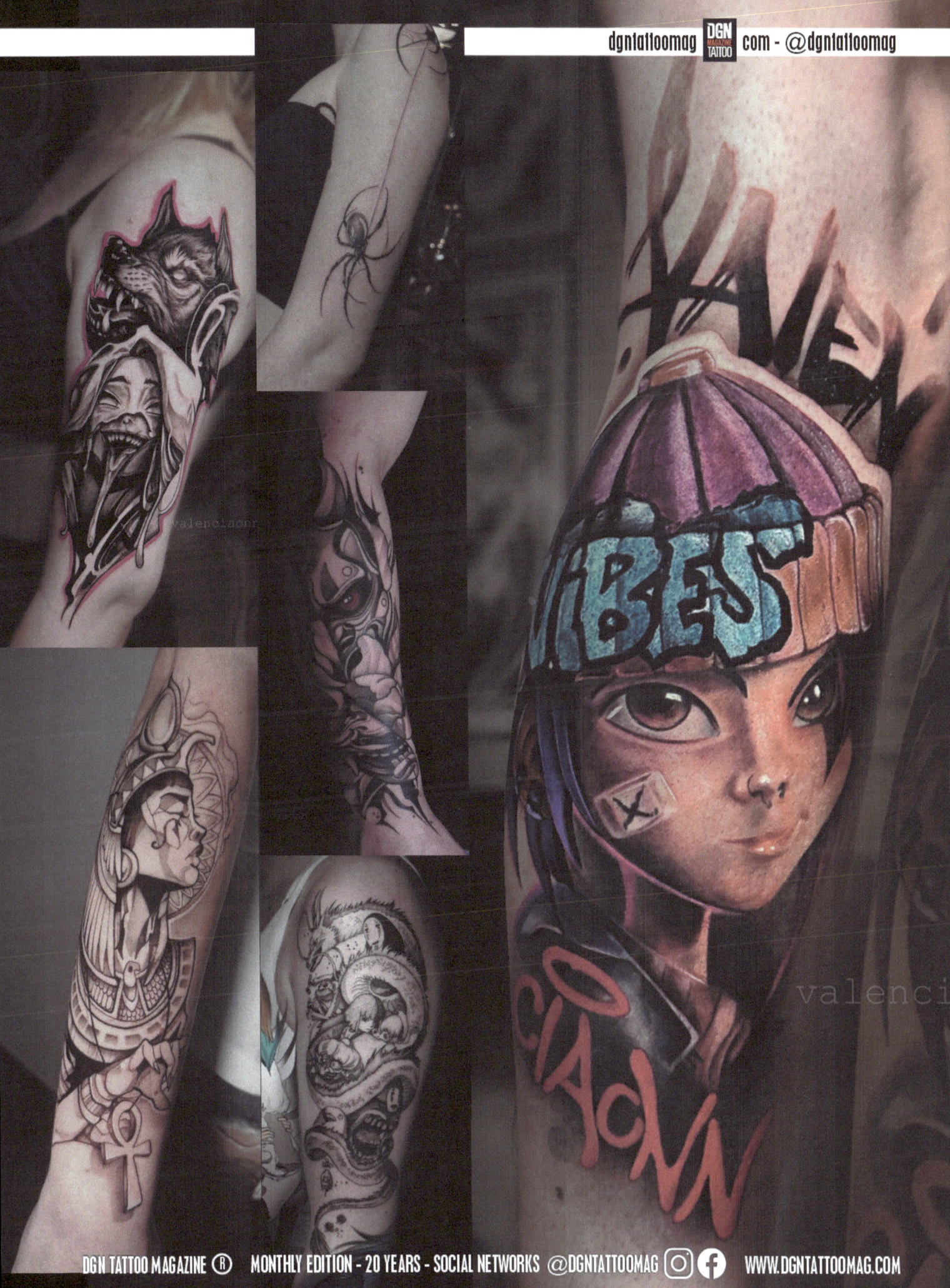

CARLOS UMBRIA

CHARLOTTE NORTH CAROLINA USA

@rafaumbria

My Name is Carlos Umbría, mostly known as Rafa. I was born on May 31 in Caracas Venezuela and I'm currently based in Charlotte, North Carolina. My love for tattooing started at a very young age when I saw my first tattoo in a public pool when I was just a kid, I was hooked ever since. As I grew older, I saw myself more and more included in the tattoo world, watching tv shows, reading magazines, hanging out at shop or going to my friend's tattoo appointments, even though I wasn't an artist and on my head I wasn't really build to draw and paint my love for body art just grew exponentially. When I was 19 years old I was studying for a college career, but then one of my friends encouraged me to pursue drawing (he actually liked my art and I honestly thought it sucked). I guess all I needed was some little push to get me going and chase my dream. I started looking and researching for a way to get an apprenticeship and all my efforts paid off when I finally found my mentor. The road hasn't been easy but after 7 years of hard work, tears, joy, ups and downs I can proudly say I'm doing the best job in the world. I love to finally fit in a business that I love, respect and appreciate, while it also shows me the love and the good things tattooing has to offer.

My work focuses on full color pieces, looking to flow and fit the part of the body accurately so it gives you the impression of the person being born with the tattoo. I love Anime and cartoons so most of my artwork rolls around that theme but I also love to do colorful, fun and dynamic bangers that create an impression and play with the viewer's view.

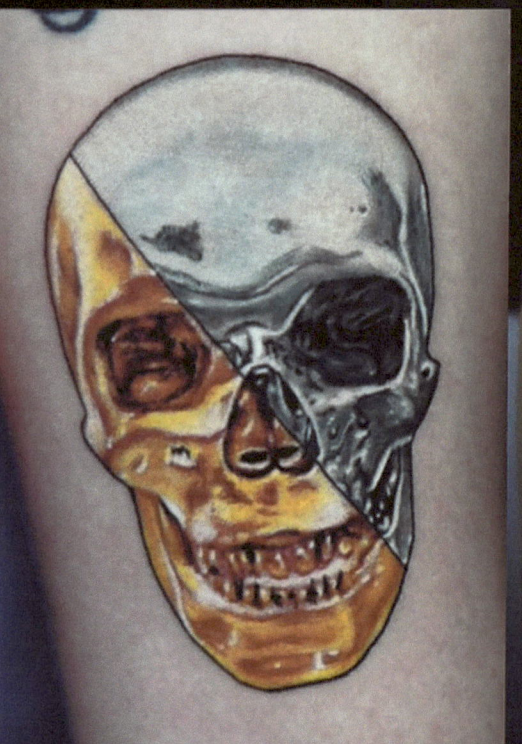
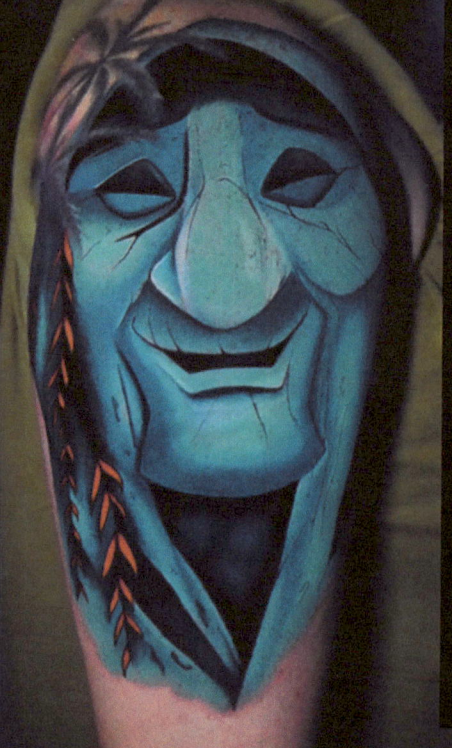
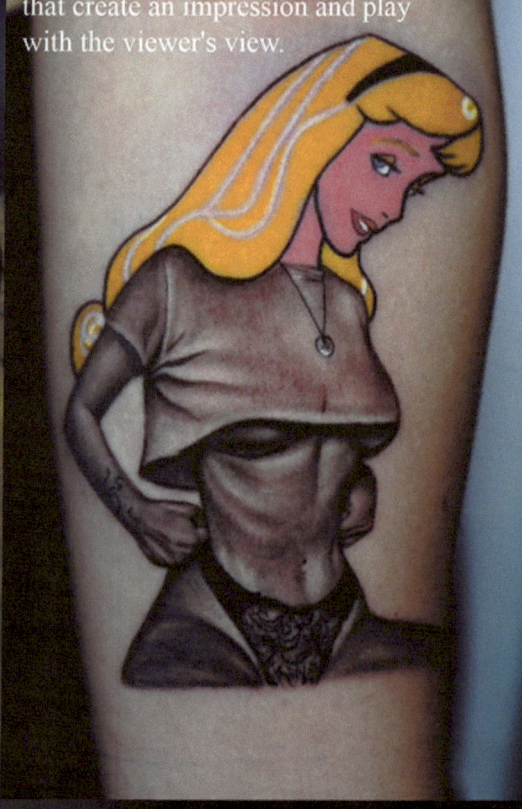

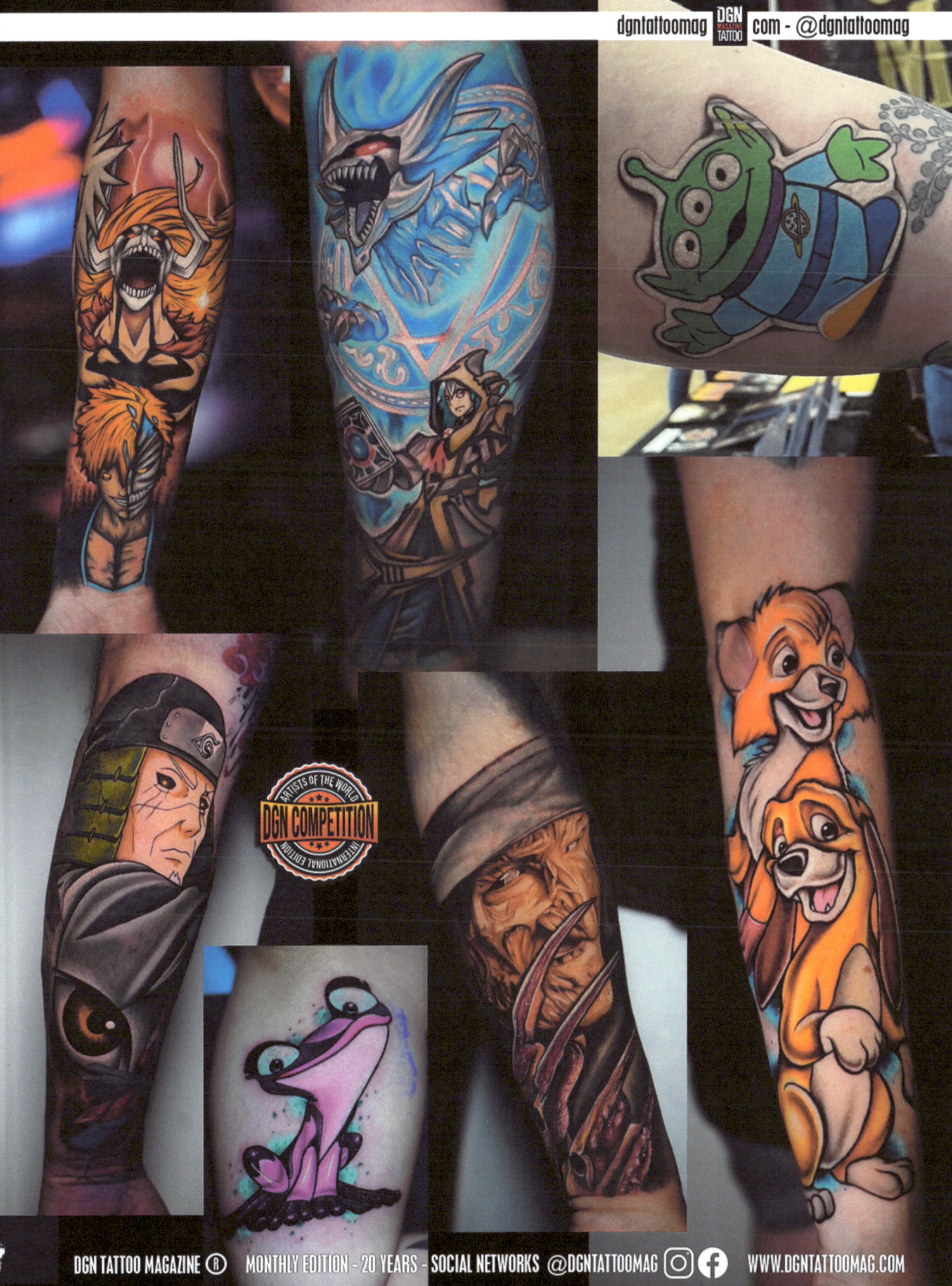

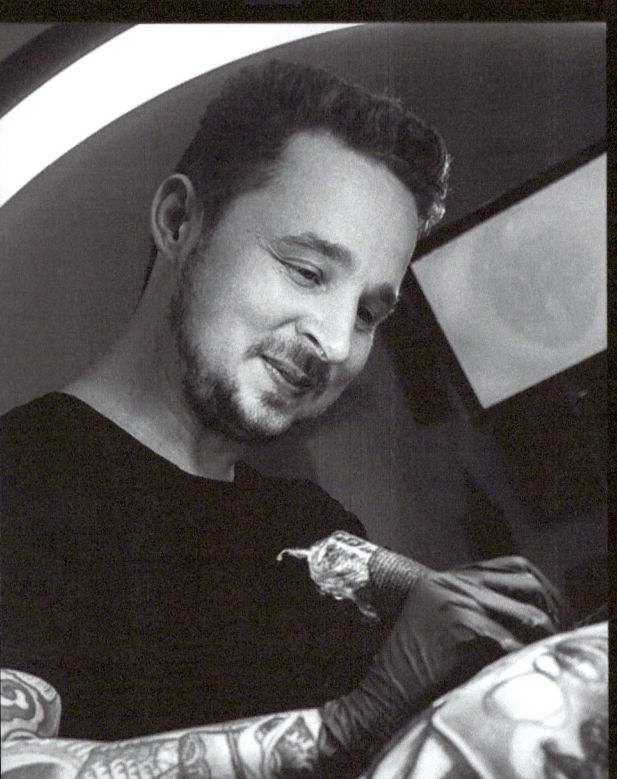

KAROL DRZEWIECKI

KONIN @defo_tattoo
phone +48 605294187

POLAND

Born and raised in the artistic hub of poland, i've always been immersed in a world of creativity. From a tender age of 4, i began painting, nurtured by the rich artistic environment of my family home. With both parents being artists, knowledge and materials were always at my fingertips, fostering my early artistic development.

After completing my education at the academy of fine arts in poland, i ventured into the world of tattooing. It was during my studies that i discovered the profound potential of tattoos as a form of artistic expression. Witnessing how tattoos could convey emotions, stories, and intricate designs ignited a passion within me. I realized that tattooing offered the same level of creative freedom and depth as traditional art forms.

In my tattooing journey, i seamlessly integrate traditional artistic techniques such as drawing with graphite and charcoal onto the skin of my clients. My signature style often revolves around portraying feminine figures and forms, with female nudes being a recurring theme. By infusing classical artistic elements into my tattoo designs, i aim to imbue each piece with a timeless and captivating quality, celebrating the beauty of the human body in all its diversity and grace.

Now residing in the heart of poland, i've established my own tattoo studio, defo tattoo. Here, i blend my traditional artistic background with the dynamic world of tattooing, creating unique and meaningful designs for my clients. For me, tattooing is not just a profession; it's a lifelong passion and artistic fulfillment.

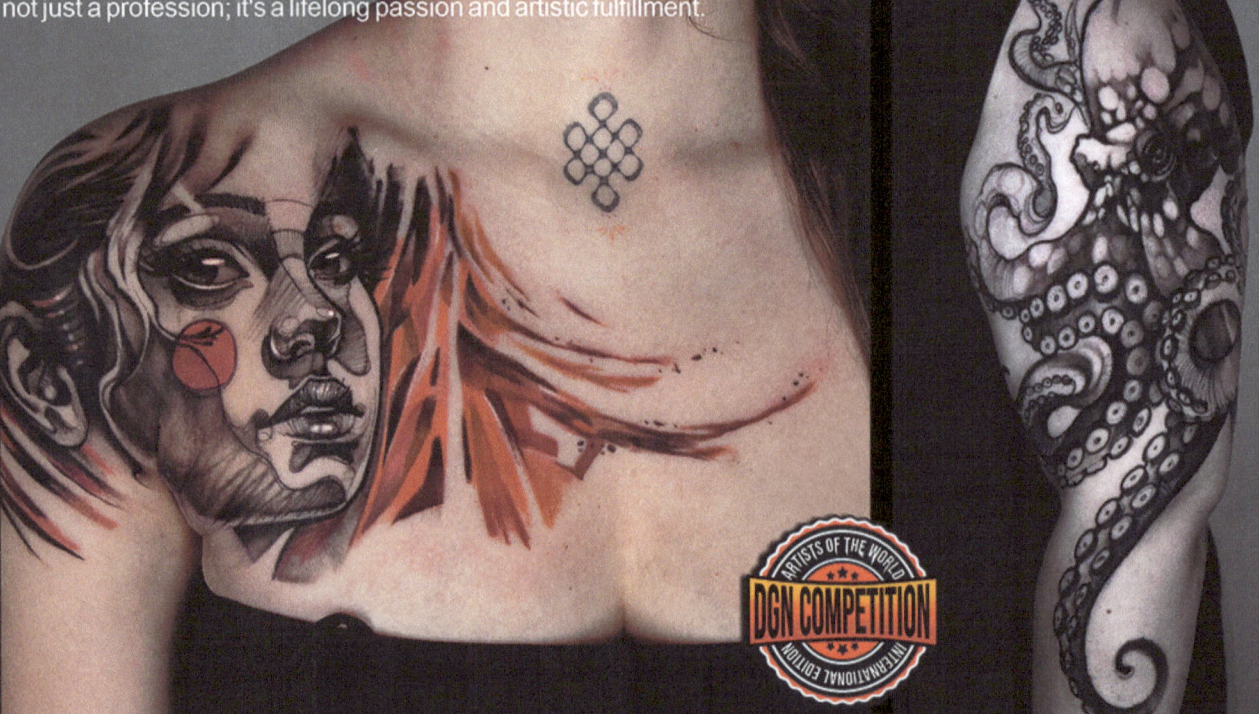

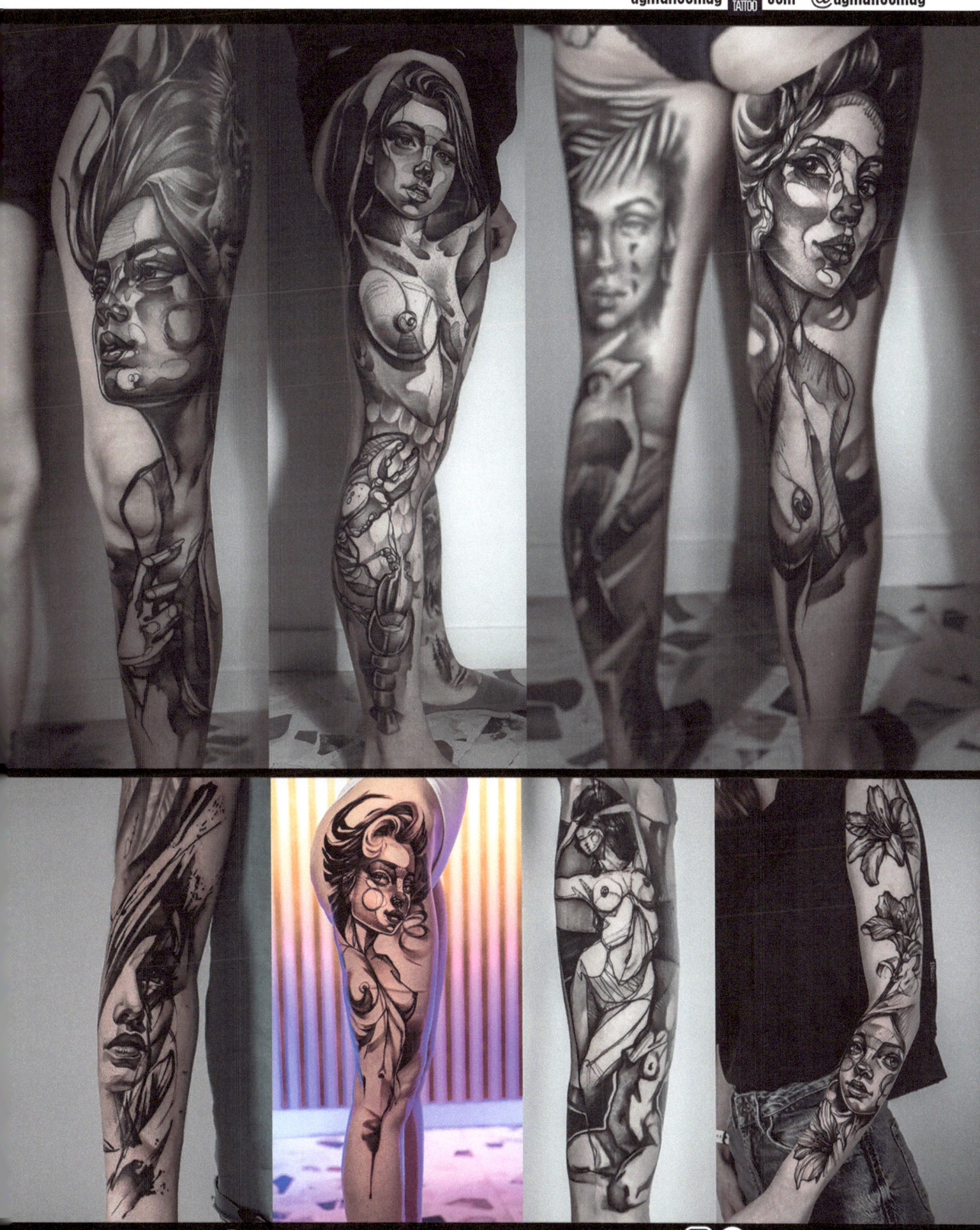

REMCO
DE VOGEL

IJMUIDEN
NETHERLANDS

@remcodevogel
Facebook: Remco de Vogel
TikTok: remcodevogel
YouTube: remcodevogel art

Remco de Vogel, from Haarlem, Netherlands, is a passionate tattoo artist who has dedicated his life to creating art on skin. From a young age, he felt an irresistible attraction to the world of tattoos and the ability to capture stories and emotions on the bodies of others.

His journey began with a modest tattoo kit at the age of 21, where he perfected his skills through experimentation and learning from the best in the industry. Driven by his love for art and his desire to connect people with meaningful designs, Remco quickly became a respected name in the tattoo community.

With an unmistakable style ranging from realistic portraits in black and grey and color to detailed sleeves, Remco captures the essence of his clients and translates it into unique and meaningful tattoos. His studio Tattoo Birdy in IJmuiden, Netherlands, serves as a sanctuary for creativity, where clients feel welcome and inspired by his passion and dedication.

Over the years, Remco de Vogel has built a loyal following, not only because of his exceptional craftsmanship but also because of his warm personality and his ability to make a lasting impact on the lives of his clients. For Remco, tattooing is not just a profession but a calling - a way to connect, tell stories, and make the world a little more beautiful, one tattoo at a time.

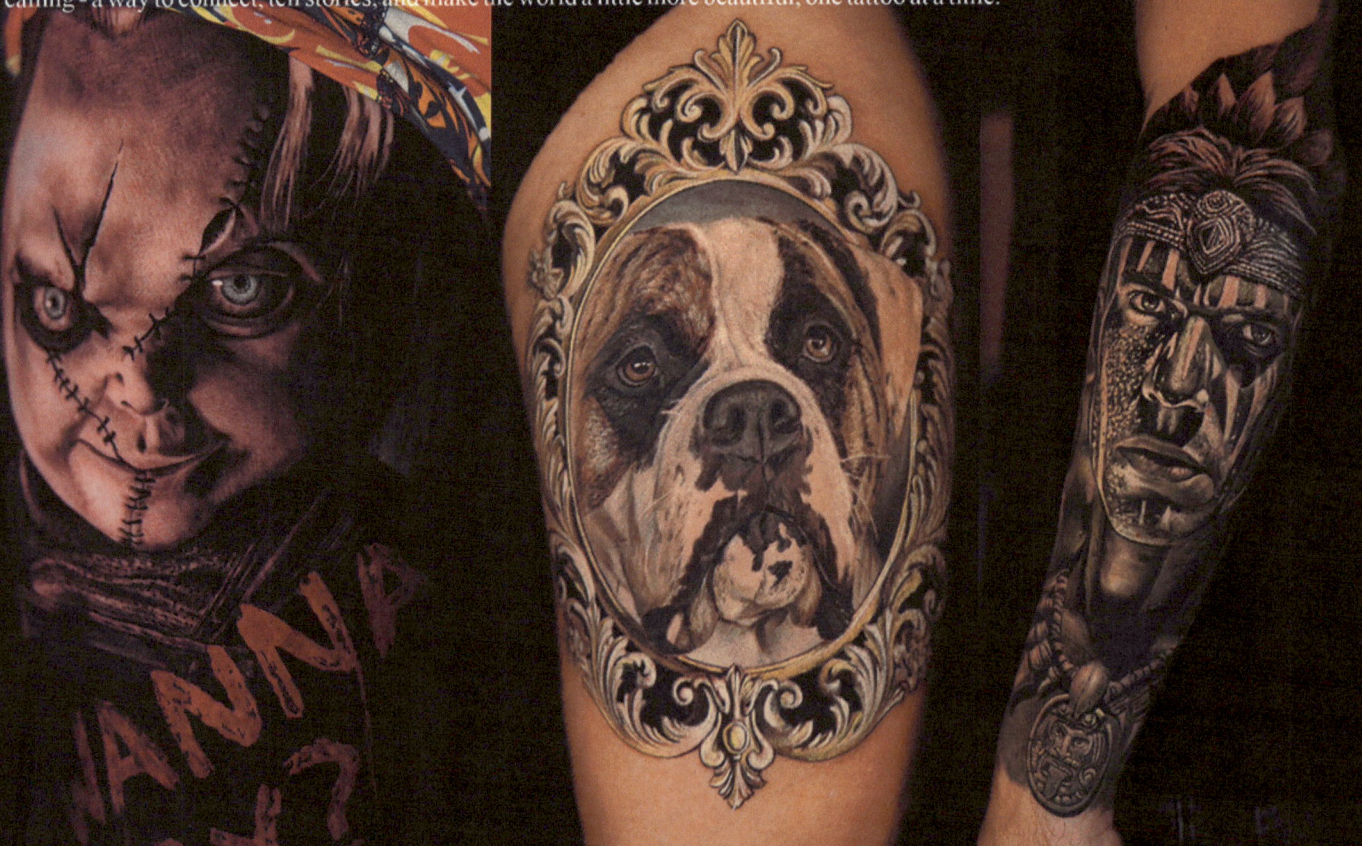

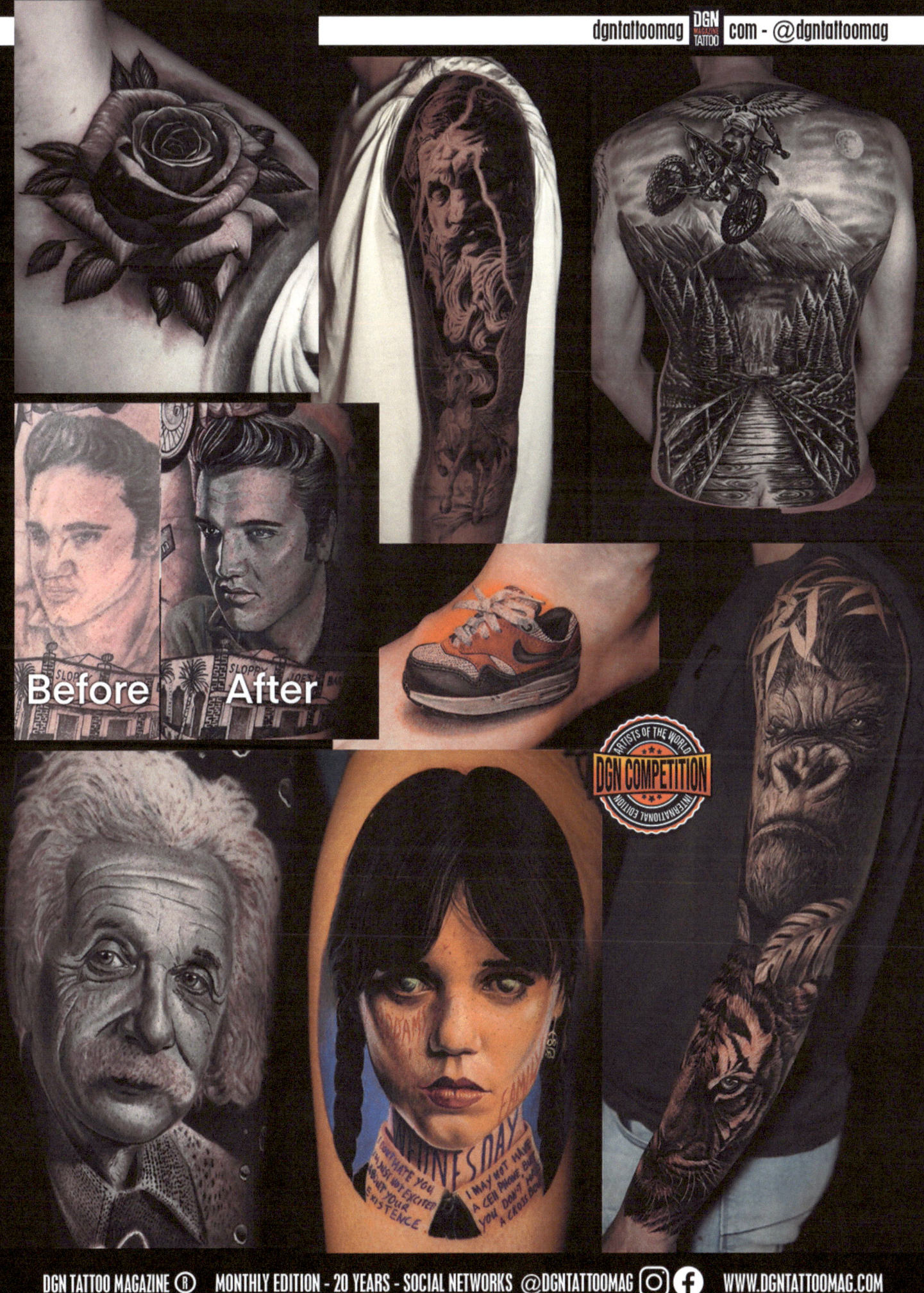

dgntattoomag DGN com - @dgntattoomag

Before After

DGN COMPETITION
ARTISTS OF THE WORLD
INTERNATIONAL EDITION

DGN TATTOO MAGAZINE ®   MONTHLY EDITION - 20 YEARS - SOCIAL NETWORKS @DGNTATTOOMAG   WWW.DGNTATTOOMAG.COM

KIRILL BALI
GRYADUNOV INDONESIA

@kirill_gryadunov_tattoo - TikTok: @kiriillgryadunov - FB: kiriillkey.gryadunov - Telegram channel: not_hungry_artist

My name is Kirill Gryadunov. I have been a tattoo artist for more than 11 years and for the last 7 years I have worked a lot in different countries, Germany, Czech, Italy, Portugal, French, Morocco, Israel, also in Asia.. I was born in a small city in Russia, in a big family. I have 2 brothers and 4 sisters, and my father is a Christian Priest.

I have drawn from my childhood, and before tattooing I worked as a theatre artist, so I know a lot about Art history. And also I have one more education as a Psychologist in university, but I have liked tattoos all my life and all my life I wanted to incorporate for the tattoo industry something unconventional, something Artistic with Art world symbols and deep meaning.

I work in my unique contemporary style that I call "Metamodern tattoo".The main thing I draw on the people is like on canvases, (randomly, expressively, thoughtfully, depending on the mood and concept) so it's a mix of many styles like: realism, graphic, watercolour, thine line, lettering etc, and I play on all of them in one concept. So my art it's a CONCEPTUAL art, I was the first person started call that style METAMODERN and I created a hashtag #metamoderntattoo so my Audience knows that I'm the founder of that style in the tattoo industry. I work a lot with many worldwide famous people (Influencers, bloggers, musicians, etc) I'm gonna be a world famous Artist! I work a lot on it!

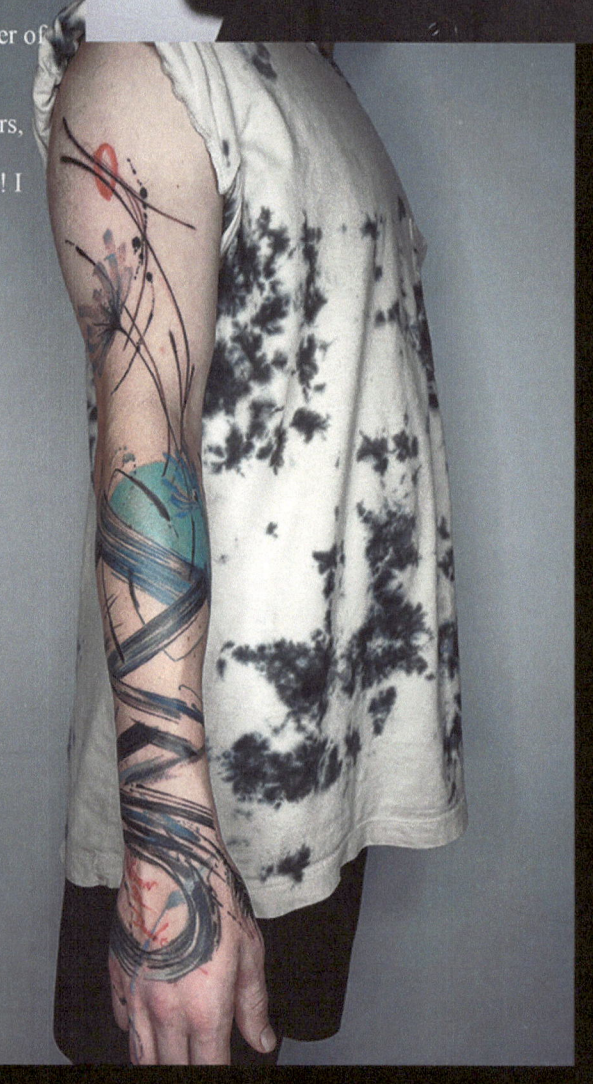

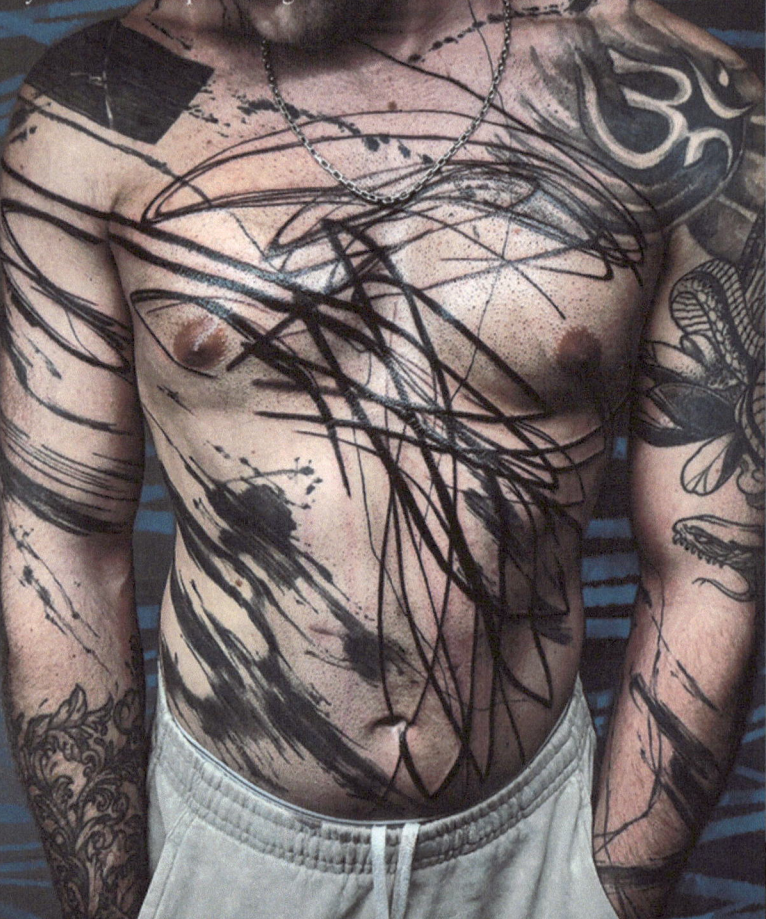

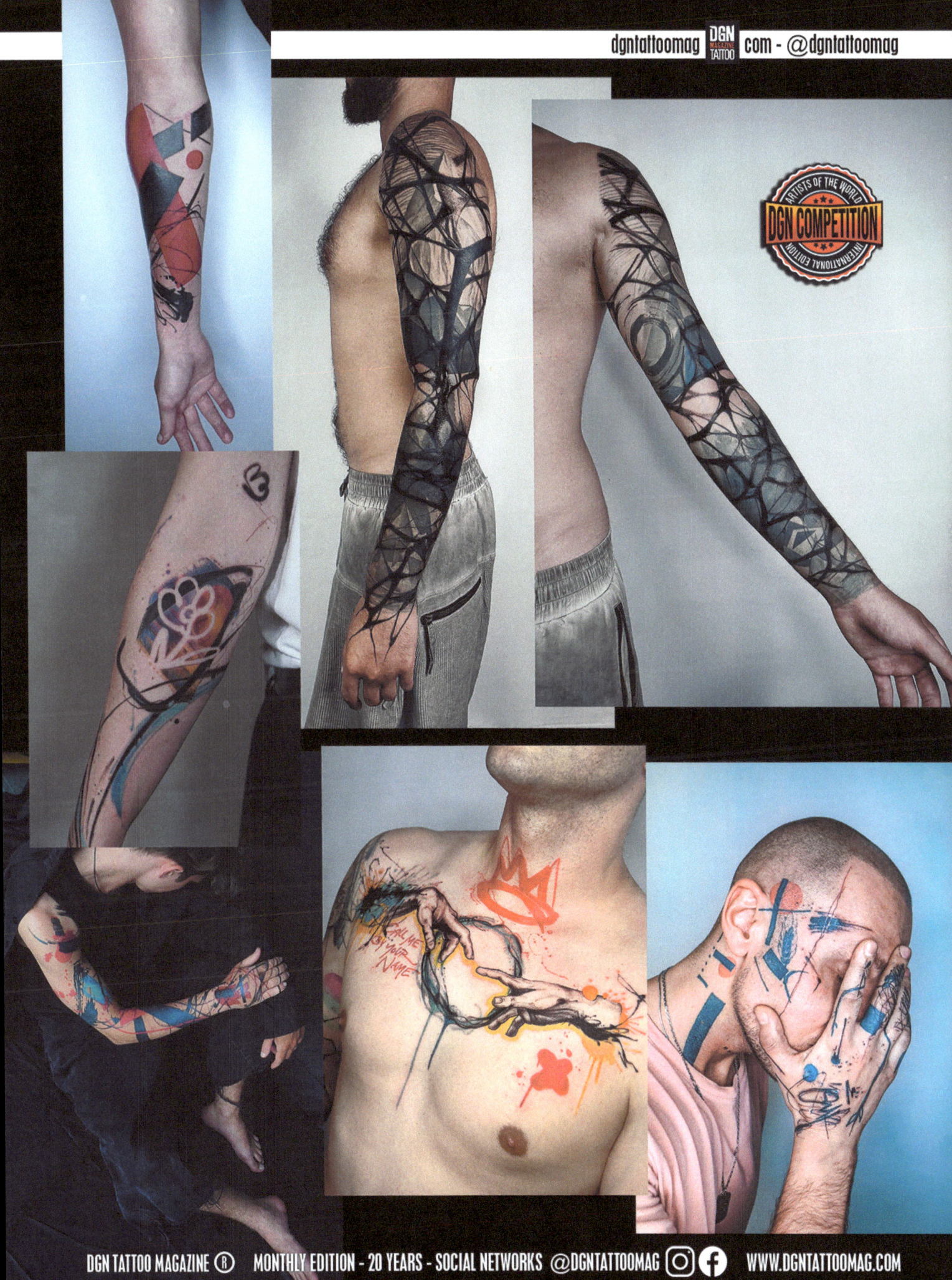

dgntattoomag DGN MAGAZINE TATTOO com - @dgntattoomag

DGN COMPETITION
ARTISTS OF THE WORLD
INTERNATIONAL EDITION

DGN TATTOO MAGAZINE ® MONTHLY EDITION - 20 YEARS - SOCIAL NETWORKS @DGNTATTOOMAG WWW.DGNTATTOOMAG.COM

LUGOVOY BOGDAN

DORTMUND GERMANY

@lugovoy_tattoo

From the age of 13, Bogdan Lugovoy knew he was going to get a tattoo, but he didn't know exactly how he was going to get there. At 17, he decided to get his first tattoo and throughout the session, he asked his tattoo artist tons of questions, and the artist was eager to answer them. Bogdan was literally obsessed with the idea of starting to tattoo. His tattoo master saw the potential in him and offered to teach him this art. After that, his life changed completely.

Bogdan Lugovoy, 29 years old, is a tattoo artist with 10 years of experience and has worked in many European tattoo studios. After the war came to Ukraine, he had to flee his country, and since then, he has been living and tattooing in Dortmund, Germany for 2 years.

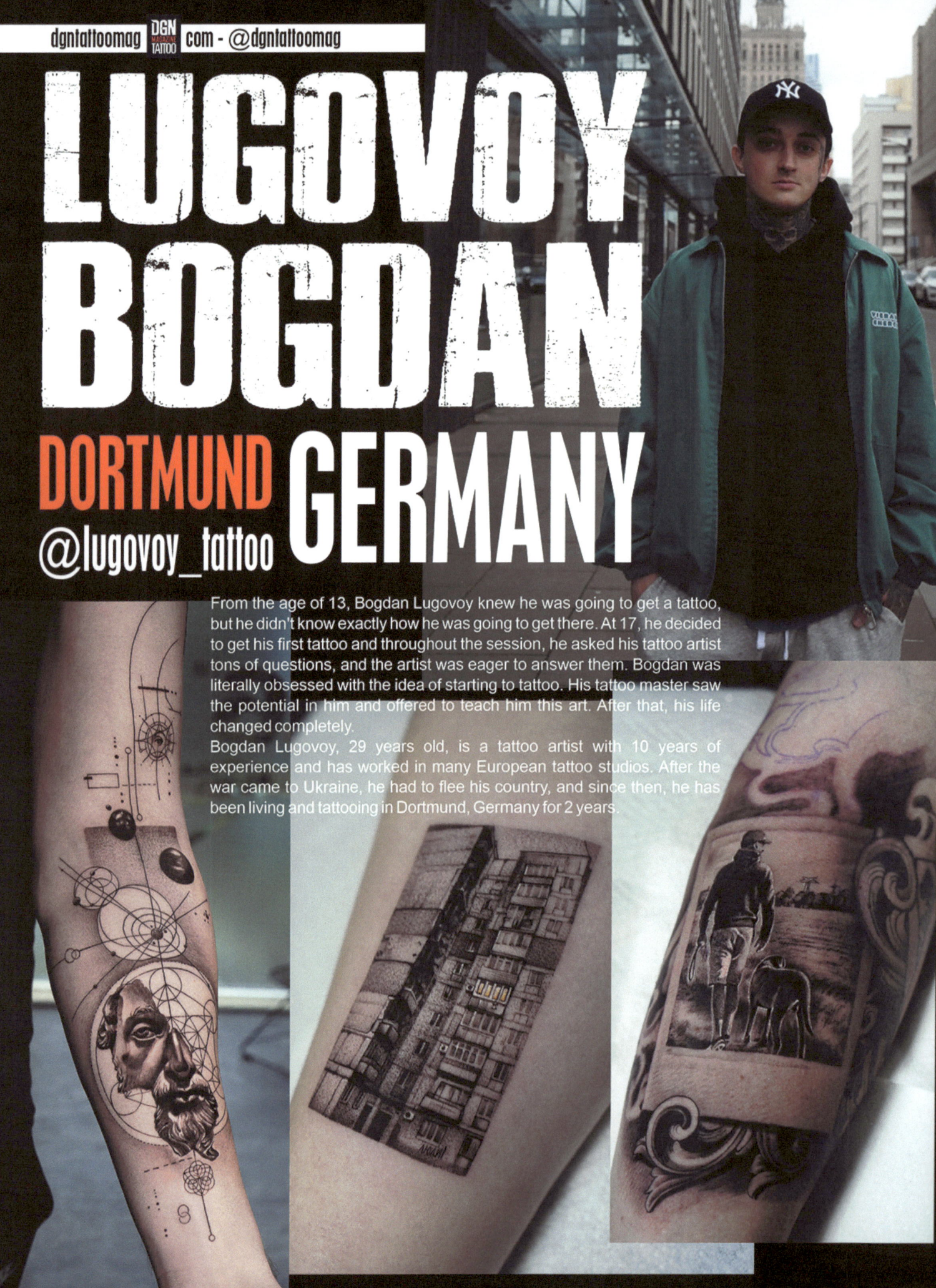

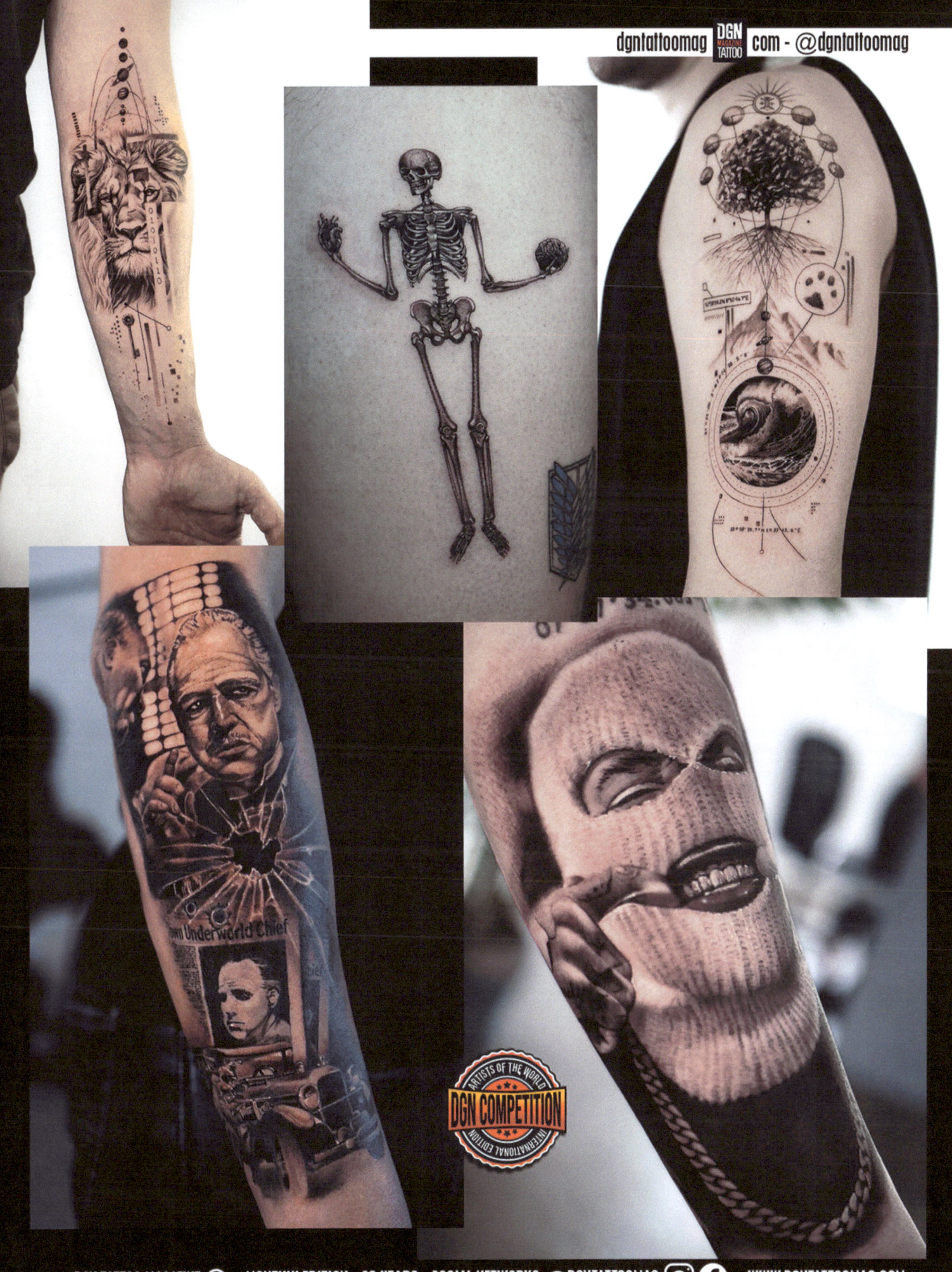

PAULA BARUC

LOS ANGELES CALIFORNIA USA

@paulabaructattoo

Hello everyone, my name is Paula Baruc, I'm Brazilian but I've been living in Los Angeles, California for quite a few years now. I've been passionate about arts since childhood, but I started my career four years ago. I had a great teacher, Filippe Art, who taught me everything. I strive to improve myself every day; art is an eternal learning process, and I aim to deliver the best to my clients because that's my commitment and what I love to do. I'm passionate about art in all its aspects, always open to trying every style and learning everything, though my main focus is Fineline and mini realism; I also love black and grey and dabble in that style too. I have my tattoo shop that welcomes clients from all over the world, Baruc Tattoo on Melrose Ave in Los Angeles. I aim to attend many tattoo conventions in the USA and other parts of the world to continually innovate my work, learn, and seek out top-quality materials. I follow the most renowned artists and try to learn a lot from them. I appreciate the opportunity.

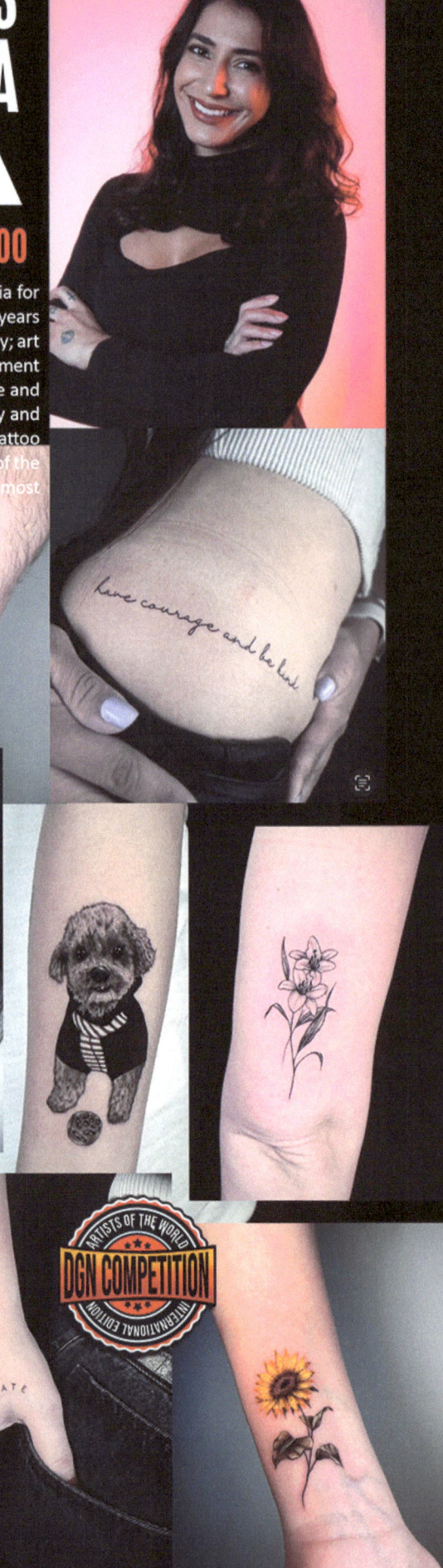

DGN COMPETITION
ARTISTS OF THE WORLD
INTERNATIONAL EDITION

VILTON GARCIA

PORTO
PORTUGAL

@viltongarciatattoo_

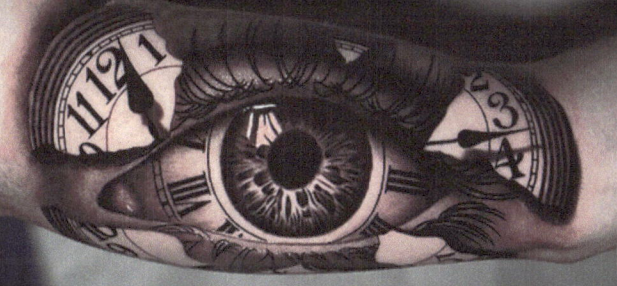

Vilton Garcia, originally from Camaquã, Brazil, discovered his passion for art at a young age, though his self-taught journey was driven by economic constraints. Overcoming initial challenges in his foray into the world of tattooing, he established his own studio in Brazil in 2021. However, in 2022, he accepted an offer to relocate to Portugal, where he continues his career as a tattoo artist, grateful for the opportunity to share his art with a wider audience.

From his childhood in Brazil to his current residence in Porto, Portugal, Vilton has demonstrated unwavering dedication to perfecting his craft. His focus on black and grey realism and his commitment to quality and originality in each tattoo reflect his passion and determination in his ongoing pursuit of excellence in the tattoo industry.

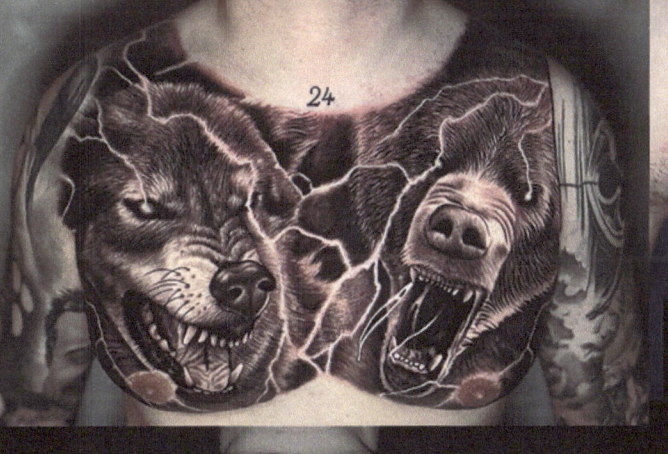

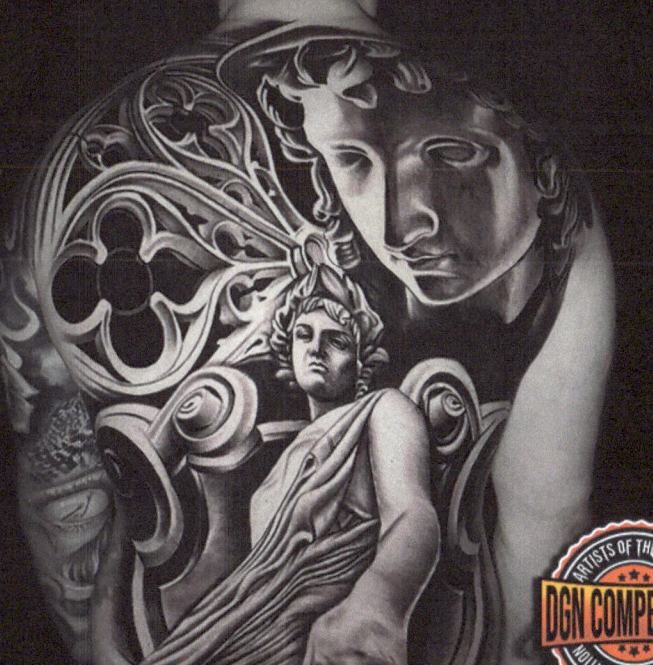

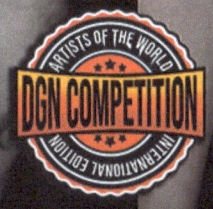

ARTISTS OF THE WORLD
DGN COMPETITION
INTERNATIONAL EDITION

 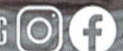

GUILLAUME PELLETIER
CANADA
QUÉBEC
@pelletier_artist_tattoo

STUDIO PELLETIER INK

I really enjoy doing realistic dark horror tattoos. I like when this trash makes people feel an emotion. I also like to make realistic projects in color or black and grey, like portraits of movie actors, sports portraits, animals, etc. But when a client chooses me as an artist and tells me he wants me to create a dark horror piece, it's like Christmas for me.

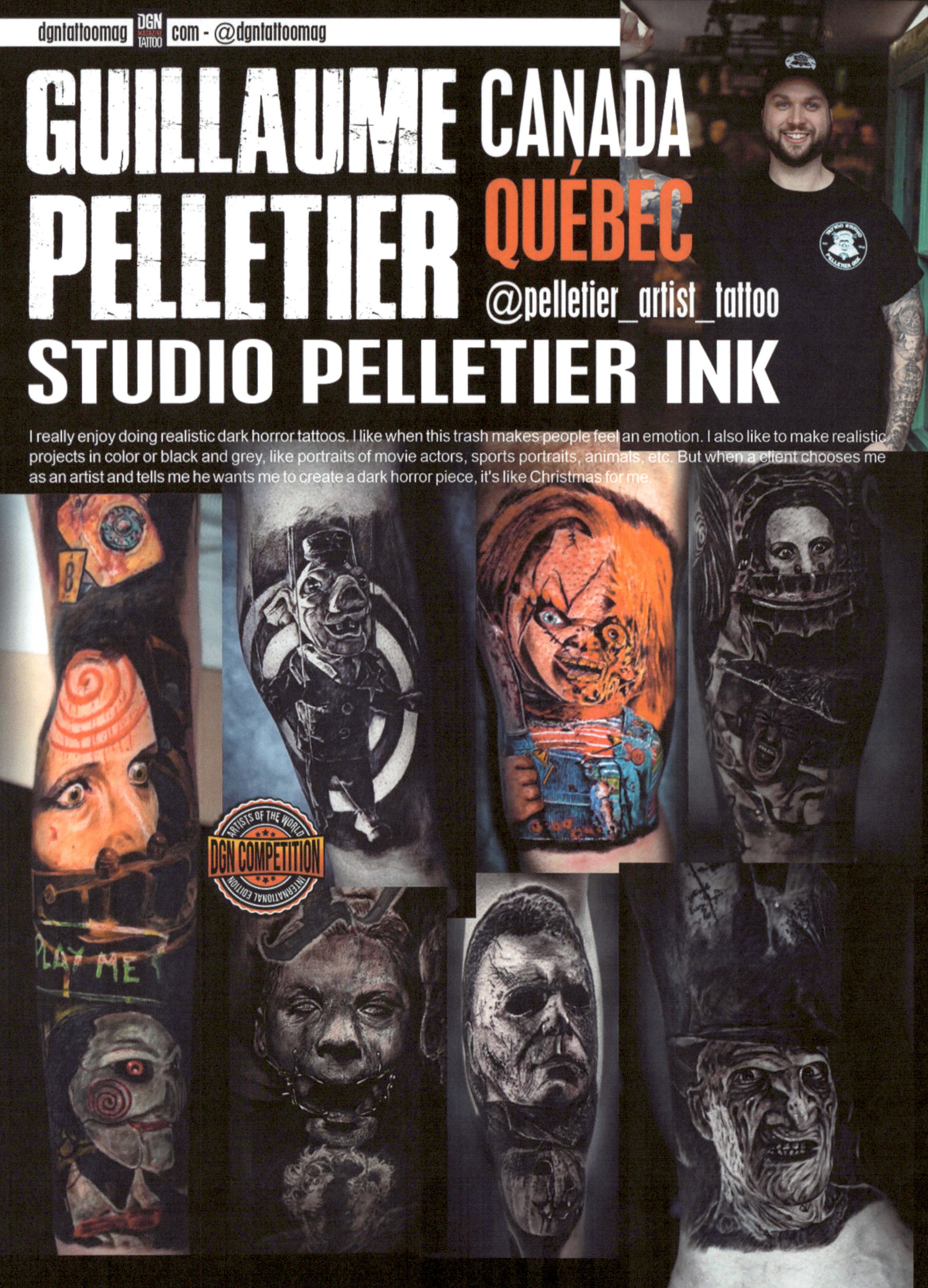

REY TEYSSE

AUSTIN TEXAS USA

@rey_teysse

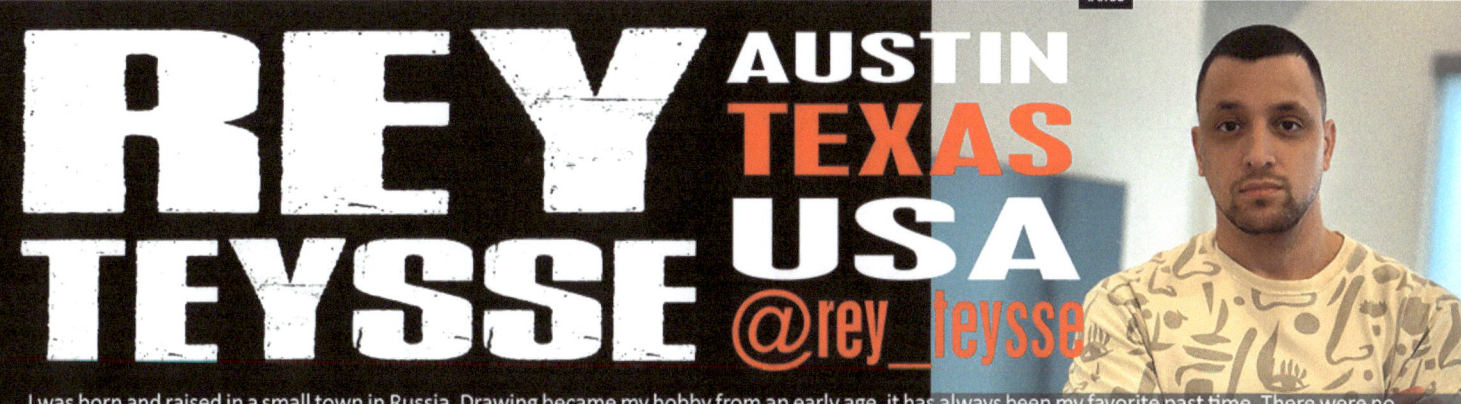

I was born and raised in a small town in Russia. Drawing became my hobby from an early age, it has always been my favorite past time. There were no people of art in my family, but it did not prevent me from enjoying drawing and progressing in my art. At the age of 14 I realized I wanted to try tattooing. By that time I had already been visiting my friends who were tattoo artists to practice and learn. On my 14th birthday I asked my father to give me tattoo equipment as a birthday present, and he didn't refuse. I purchased the equipment and started making my first steps. At first, I only did tattoos for my friends and other high school students.

When I started college, I moved to a big city and continued tattooing. Eventually, it became my primary job. Many years have passed, and I found my calling in black work. I love transforming drawings to reimagine them as lines of different thickness. I especially enjoy depicting marine creatures, octopuses in particular.

In 2018 we moved to the US with my wife. To this day, I continue pursuing my favorite job, continue progressing, and have no intention of stopping.

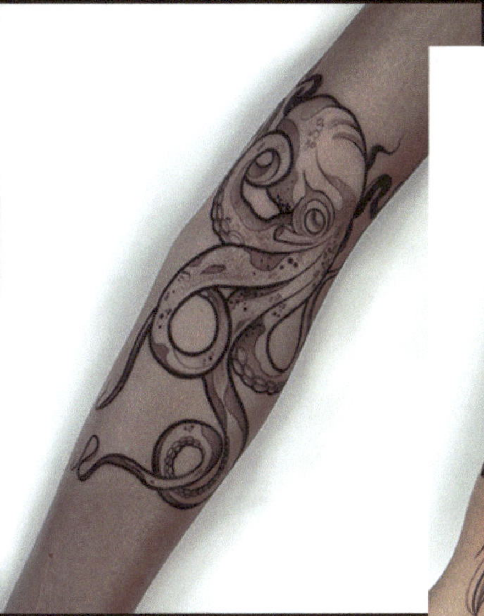

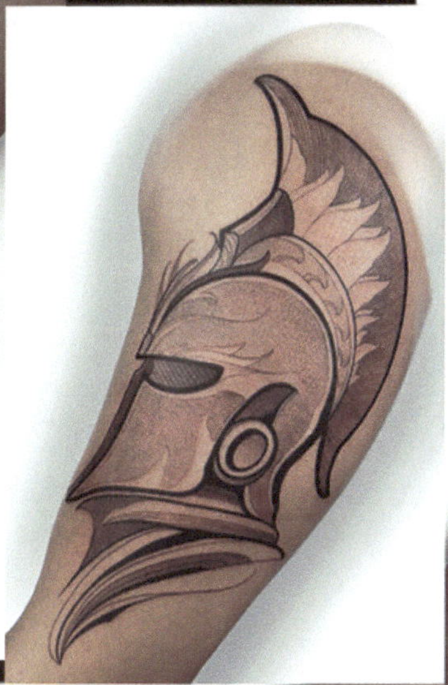

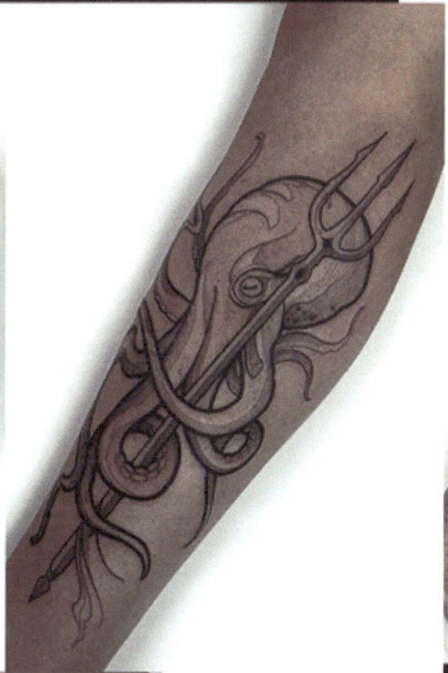

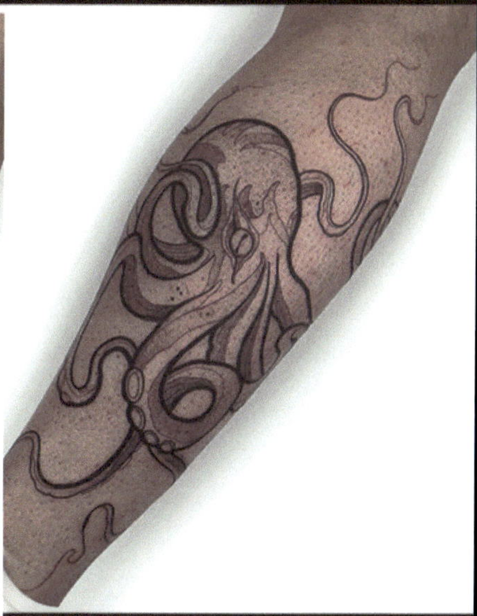

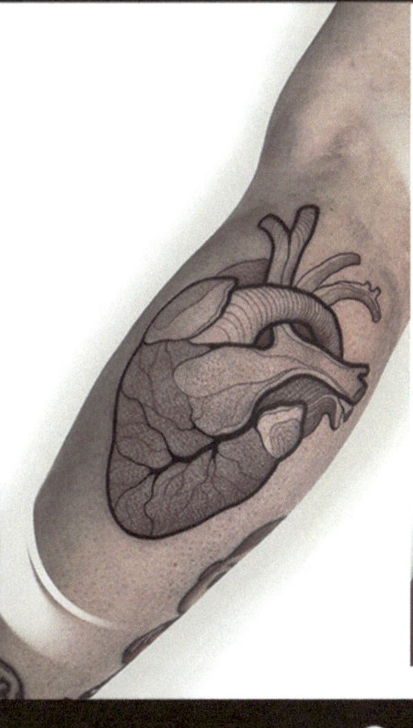

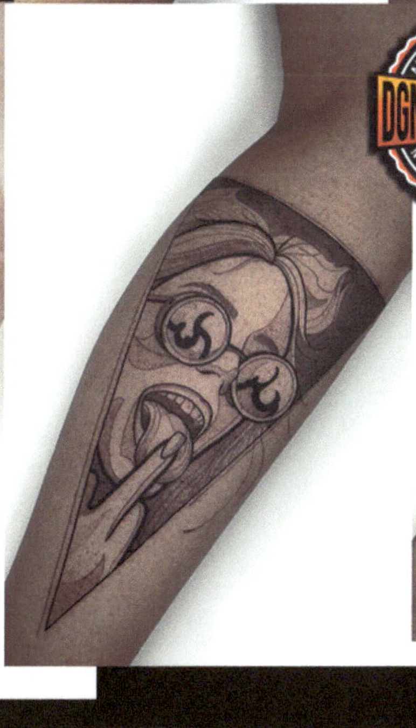

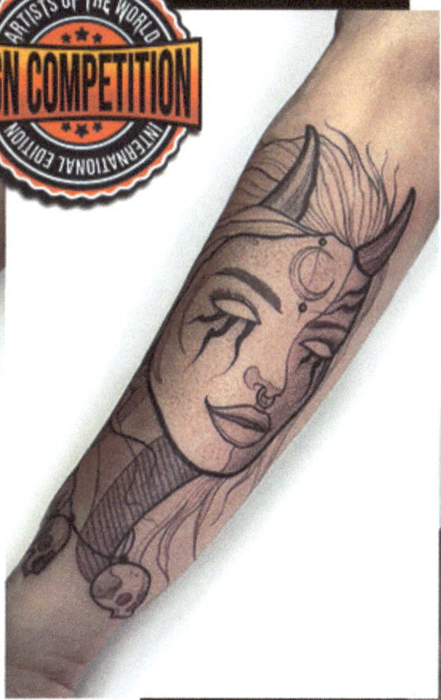

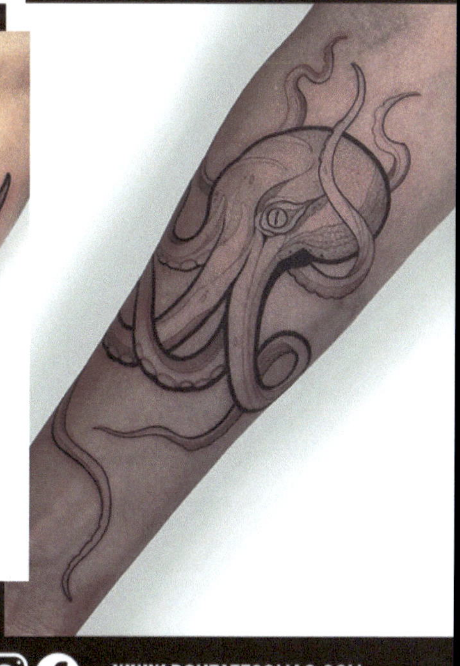

DGN TATTOO MAG

XX YEAR - MONTHLY EDITION
MAY 2024 - #174

DIRECTOR:

Sebastian Harbaruk
eventosdgn@hotmail.com

WEB PRODUCER AND EDITOR

Ibrahin Harbaruk / Lautaro Tinti

DESIGN AND EDITORIAL PRODUCTION OF

De La Madre Producciones
delamadre@gmail.com

PHOTOGRAPHY

Leyla Ferreyra
ph.editorial@dgn.com
Pancha Carolga Harbaruk
pancha@gmail.com

TRANSLATIONS

Flor Antonietti
florantonietti@yahoo.com.ar

ADMINISTRATION

Pablo Di Gruccio
pablodigruccio@gmail.com

MARKETING AND SALES

Estrella Ferreyra
dgntattoomag@hotmail.com
+549 11 30073999
Facebook.com/dgntattoomag

SUBSCRIPTIONS

dgntattoomag@gmail.com

DGN TATTOO MAGAZINE
is a registered trademark

CONTACTS

USA +1 (213) 633-7712
LATAM +54 9 11-3007-3999
eventosdgn@hotmail.com

FOLLOW US ON

Instagram/dgntattoomag
Face/dgn-tattoo-magazine

WWW.DGNTATTOOMAG.COM

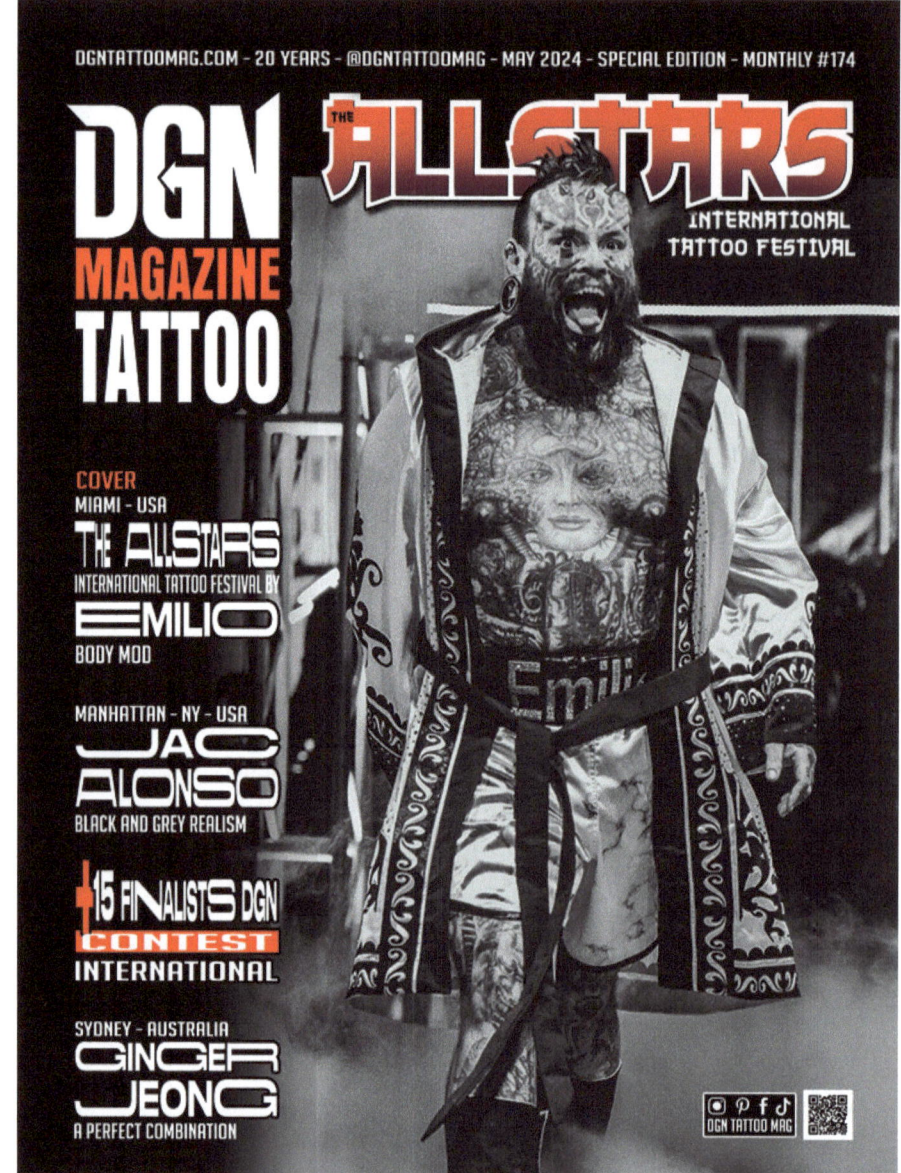

DGNTATTOOMAG.COM - 20 YEARS - @DGNTATTOOMAG - MAY 2024 - SPECIAL EDITION - MONTHLY #174

DGN MAGAZINE TATTOO

THE ALLSTARS
INTERNATIONAL TATTOO FESTIVAL

COVER
MIAMI - USA
THE ALLSTARS
INTERNATIONAL TATTOO FESTIVAL BY
EMILIO
BODY MOD

MANHATTAN - NY - USA
JAC ALONSO
BLACK AND GREY REALISM

15 FINALISTS DGN
CONTEST
INTERNATIONAL

SYDNEY - AUSTRALIA
GINGER JEONG
A PERFECT COMBINATION

DGN TATTOO MAG

Editor:
Sebastian Harbaruk
dgntattoomag@gmail.com

Editorial Creative Laboratory:
DGN TATTOO
Laprida 151, B1832HOC
Green Corridor Canning / San Vicente
Country Club S/N - AR

International Distribution:

Amazon and Kindle © 1996-2023, Amazon.com, Inc. or affiliates. All rights reserved.
Amazon and Kindle are registered trademarks of Amazon.com Inc. or affiliates.

Issuu, Inc.

131 Lytton Avenue, Palo Alto, California, Estados Unidos.
Enriching lives through meaningful content since 2006.
www.issuu.com www.facebook.com/issuu
© issuu Inc. 131 Lytton Ave., Palo Alto, CA 94301

© DGN TATTOO MAG.

The opinions expressed in the articles do not necessarily reflect the point of
view of DGN TATTOO MAGAZINE
the responsibility for their content corresponds to their authors. The publisher is not responsible
for the material delivered by the client, photographs of advertisements and signed notes

www.ingramcontent.com/pod-product-compliance
Lightning Source LLC
Chambersburg PA
CBHW042028230526
45474CB00006B/38